WRITING

A GUIDE FOR STUDENTS

by
Michael Newby

with

Janet Brennan
Diane O'Sullivan
Nicholas Potter
Peter Williams

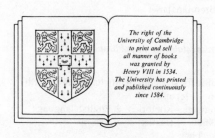

The right of the
University of Cambridge
to print and sell
all manner of books
was granted by
Henry VIII in 1534.
The University has printed
and published continuously
since 1584.

CAMBRIDGE UNIVERSITY PRESS

Cambridge
New York   Port Chester
Melbourne   Sydney

*Our thanks to Phil Aubrey
and to students and colleagues
at the
West Glamorgan Institute of Higher Education,
Swansea*

Published by the Press Syndicate of the University of Cambridge
The Pitt Building, Trumpington Street, Cambridge CB2 1RP
40 West 20th Street, New York, NY 10011, USA
10 Stamford Road, Oakleigh, Melbourne 3166, Australia

First published 1989

Printed in Great Britain at The Bath Press, Avon

British Library cataloguing in publication data
Newby, Michael
    Writing : a guide for students.
    1. Schools. Students. Writing skills
    I. Title   II. Brennan, Janet
    808'.042

Library of Congress cataloging-in-publication data

Newby, Michael.
    Writing: a guide for students/by Michael Newby with
    Janet Brennan . . . [et al.].
    1. English language – Rhetoric.   2. English language –
    Grammar – 1950-   I. Title.
    PE1408.N426   1989
    808'.042 – dc20

ISBN 0 521 37930 x

PN

Contents

LAURIE TAYLOR

Professor Lapping! Might I have a word?

Ah, Abdul. Keeping well? Settling in nicely? Jolly good. Must dash.

Abd*ou*, Professor Lapping. Abd*ou*.

Ah yes. Well, Abdou, what seems to be the trouble? Good heavens, is that the time?

It's my essay, Professor Lapping. I'm afraid I do not understand all your comments.

Cultural differences, Abdou. A grey old world without them.

I do not understand, for example, the meaning of this 'Sp'.

Spelling, Abdou.

Spelling?

That's it. Glance across the line and you'll see I've underlined the misspelt word so you can go and look it up and get it right next time. Simple as that.

I see. And then *here*, and *here*, and *here*, you have written something which looks like 'Pu'.

Punctuation, Abdou. Punctuation. Some basic fault or other. Could be almost anything: need for a comma, incorrect use of a colon, faulty apostrophes. Try reading your work out loud to yourself. That often gives a clue. Now, I really must dash.

I see. And then I do not understand all these other signs – the upside down 'v's.

Quite straightforward. They mean something or other has been missed out – a word, an idea, a reference. Whatever.

Ah. And then there are these question marks. All by themselves.

**They mean that I'm not too clear about what you're saying – that it is, *literally*, *ques*_ *tionable. Now . . .*

And then I do not quite make sense of your other comments. On this page you say 'Are you sure?', over here you say 'Really?' and 'Does this follow?', and here on the last page 'Can this be true?'

Should have thought they spoke for themselves, Abdou. Good heavens, is that the time.

Professor Lapping, perhaps I am taking a little longer to settle down than some other overseas students, but I do wonder if your marking might ever be a little more – well – helpful?

'Helpful', Abdou?

Well, instead of saying over and over again that my things were wrong – could you ever spare a moment to tell me what would be *right*?

Good God, Abdou! Whatever next? Spoonfeeding?

Laurie Taylor

Introduction

This book is for people who have to write as part of their college course. If you are one of them, you will be asked by your lecturers to complete written assignments, many of which will be graded and will count towards your final assessment. What's more, you will probably have to take written examinations at the end of your course, and maybe along the way as well. It is obviously very important that, no matter how well you understand your subject, you don't let the way you write damage your chances of success when it should be doing just the opposite. Many students can find writing in college a daunting prospect, and yet have nowhere to turn for help. If you are one of them, this book has been written for you.

Other students come to college as 'good writers' already. If you think that you write well (and have, perhaps, been complimented on your writing by teachers and others) the book may still be useful to you. This is because you will almost certainly find the kinds of writing required of you in college set you new challenges, requiring you to meet different and more testing standards than anything you met in school.

Increasingly, students come to college not from school but from the adult world of work and family. Perhaps you are one of them. If so, you will probably have to learn all over again what it feels like to be a student, and writing in an educational setting is something you won't have done for some years. For you, too, this book should help you get back into the frame of mind you'll need for writing in college.

Few college lecturers see it as their job to give writing

1

lessons. Not unreasonably, some say that all that should have been sorted out at school. Others can see that there are special problems associated with writing in college which schools can hardly be expected to have taught. Nonetheless, they have little time to help their students solve them. Their work, after all, is to teach the subject and to respond to what their students write for them primarily from the point of view of facts, ideas, processes and relationships; not the writing itself. They may comment on the writing. They may tell students that they should improve their writing. They may even suggest the areas in which improvements could be made. However, they will leave it to the students themselves to see to those improvements. If this happens to you, then this book will be a place from which to make a start.

There's another important reason why it will repay you to give careful attention to your writing while at college. Writing is a way of slowing down and making more clear the process of thinking itself. Good writing is a means to good thinking. If your writing is not of the quality you would like it to achieve, it will mean that your thinking cannot find the precision and clarity of expression which it deserves. This is the most important reason of all for learning to write as well as you can. As it happens, it is also a major reason why writing is required of so many students in so many different subjects when they come to college: it is to help them think better.

One thing may surprise you: that although the bulk of this book is about writing, it also contains sections on reading, talking and listening. If so, remember that this is a book about writing in college – and college is a place where people listen, talk and read as well as write. Indeed, most of the writing you will do in college will arise out of those other ways of using language, or will lead back into them. How else will you find the things you wish to write about than by reading, listening and talking?

Learning to write well is a process which begins for most people when they go to primary school – and continues throughout their lives. Even the most experienced writer will tell you that this process of learning never ends. However, it can be interrupted if you don't practise writing regularly, and it stands to reason that the more you write the more fluent you will grow. One of the many advantages of going to college is that it gives you the chance to write seriously and often.

Whatever else you have achieved by the end of your course, you should have become a better writer.

However, writing well is more than simply a matter of constant practice. It also needs conscious attention, and from two sources. One source will be that of your readers, whose responses can help you see with more clarity how your writing succeeds, as well as where its weaknesses may lie. The other source of attention must come from you. By looking calmly and honestly at your own writing, by attending to what your writing is expressing, you will find that it comes into ever-clearer focus. Once you see it more clearly, you can control it more surely. The image which may before have been a blur will take on a new sharpness. Some of the lenses you will need are in this book.

The book also asks you to consider your attitudes to writing. Attitudes matter as well as skills and experience. So read the next few pages and give yourself some encouragement and reassurance. . . .

Attitudes

Writing is a normal human activity

There is nothing to stop any normal person from learning to write well. Writing is like talking: a natural ability – once you have learned how to do it. It develops with use in the right environment. If you are 'normal' – that is, if there is nothing wrong with the parts of you which are needed for writing – then you can learn how to write better. Even if there really is something wrong (which is most unlikely), don't give up hope: the chances are that you can still improve considerably.

Problems you almost certainly don't have

'Something wrong' means that you may have a condition which might be hindering you in your efforts to write properly: maybe trouble in the muscles controlling your hand or arm, or eyesight difficulties which make it hard for you to focus for long on the page, or perhaps neurological problems which get in the way of good writing because your brain finds it hard to translate the words in your head to the correct marks on the page. It is extremely unlikely that this is the case. However, if you are seriously worried that there may be something wrong, go and see your doctor, who can arrange for you to have tests to find out exactly what the problem might be.

5

Are you out of practice?

Assuming nothing physical or neurological is preventing you from writing well, remember that another important reason why people don't write as well as they could is because they don't have much practice. Like any other ability, writing becomes easier the more you do it. If, for example, you have come to college after two years of studying 'A' levels (like Maths) which do not give many opportunities for writing, it may be difficult to sit down and write an essay with the same ease as people who have written them once a week for several years.

Do you like writing?

Failure to write well can also create emotional problems and these can obscure a writer's abilities. Think how much of your writing is connected with study – writing which will be read by a lecturer and probably given a grade. This is an unrelaxed situation in which to write, especially if your previous offerings have been criticised for poor writing. The result could be a build-up of anxiety, growing to the point at which you come actually to dislike writing, feeling ill-at-ease each time you have to commit your ideas to paper.

Your ideas do matter

If this is the case, then part of the solution will be for you to develop a more positive, less tense attitude to your writing in college. If your ideas are important to you, then they will probably communicate your sense of conviction to a reader, and certainly be far more interesting to read as well. So do not be ashamed of what you want to say through your writing. This will, in turn, help you to be more relaxed, more confident about writing, and this change of attitude could help you write better.

Your language is very complicated

Human language – the medium in which you express your ideas – is a set of inter-related systems of tremendous complexity: systems of sound, structure, meaning, style, etc. (Imagine the problems any other living creature would have in trying to read this page without a language system like yours.) Don't be hesitant, therefore, about your language. You may need to practise new skills to make your written language even more useful to you than it already is, but your language now is well-established, extremely complex and flexible from constant use. What may be needed now is for you to polish small areas of it, and develop some new ones which are particularly appropriate for the writing you have to do in college.

Writing is complicated too

No-one is saying that good writing is easy. Complex behaviour seldom is. However, it is useful to remember the differences between writing *problems* and writing *difficulties*. The first you can do something about; the second are what make writing so interesting and satisfying (and sometimes infuriating) a part of life. Just as language is a set of inter-related systems, so writing is a complicated set of related skills, ones in which you have already become very proficient. This must be so if you remember how far you have come since you made the first shaky scribbles on a piece of paper in the infants' class. Whatever the problems you may now have, though they may be annoying and even worrying ones, they are insignificant in comparison to the problems you have already solved.

You are not alone

Most people find writing difficult sometimes, even those who write for a living. Few professional writers could honestly say they never needed to check a spelling in the dictionary; disagreement exists among fluent writers about the exact use of commas; clever people can write tortured, laborious prose which lacks clarity and sends the reader to sleep; professionals can get 'writer's block', where the words and ideas just won't come. All these problems are additional to the in-built difficulties of writing itself, difficulties involving how best to launch an argument or present information, which way round the parts of a sentence need to be to make the strongest impact on the reader, which word to choose for maximum effect, what style to adopt, and so on.

7

People can enjoy writing

Even for accomplished writers, writing can sometimes be difficult. However, it should wherever possible be a pleasure as well, particularly in the careful expression of your ideas in the kind of written assignments required of you as a student. Many people would argue that it is only by carefully writing it down that you can really decide what it is you think and know about the issues and ideas you are studying. The process of learning through writing can be exciting and rewarding – every bit as much as *talking* about the subjects you have chosen to study with other people who share the same interests.

'Rules'

Don't worry about occasional references in this book to 'grammar' or to 'rules'. The fact is that, without them, making and receiving spoken or written language would be quite impossible. However, people don't learn their language by first learning the rules and afterwards applying them. Instead, they hear it, start to copy it, sort out its rules and regularities, try it out for themselves, make useful mistakes, see how the world-out-there responds . . . and in this way, gradually, they acquire the language habit. Later on, they do the same with reading and writing. At first, these habits need only be of use in the home, the local community, the school. As the years go by, however, new habits must be picked up to meet more complex language demands. In college, you may need to acquire still more – and perhaps lose a few as well – to meet the sometimes specialised language requirements of your own course of study. Like most rules and conventions shared by members of a community, language rules are necessary to ensuring that messages can be clearly delivered, received and understood. But always remember: people learn habits, not rules. 'Grammar' does no more than describe the habits you already know – the rules which you share with all other users of your language.

Writing is power

Writing is a way of preserving language in space and time. As human societies developed, those who could read and write tended to hold most influence. Written language was the property of the privileged and powerful; the law-makers, the spiritual leaders, the thinkers and changers. It is still the case that, in some societies in the world, many people are illiterate and have little power in consequence. However, in advanced societies it has become increasingly important for all people to share in this power; to be able to make their language travel in space and to preserve it in time by being able to write it down.

In the context of education, you need to write above all to help you think, and to demonstrate that thinking to other people. Be it the scribbled notes you write in a lecture, the carefully-researched dissertation you prepare over several months of study, or all the other kinds of written language you will make during your college career, writing gives you more control over your own ideas and understanding. This control is power.

*

The pages you have been reading were written on a word-processor and then changed several times, each time allowing the writer to correct mistakes, change words, sentences and even paragraphs until it seemed he would probably not be able to express the ideas any better. (You may disagree and think they could be expressed far more successfully than they have been.) The first version – called, technically, a first 'draft' – started from almost nothing: just an idea that a book to help people who have to write in college might be more useful if it started with *attitudes*, since people have to be in the right frame of mind before they can start trying to improve their skills. As the writing took shape, gradually a set of ideas came out onto the page and, after a while, seemed to come to a natural conclusion.

The next stage was to read them through to see if they made sense. Some of them did but others weren't as clear as they should have been. The paragraph headed 'Your ideas do matter' was particularly difficult and it ended up almost completely re-written from its original form. At the same time, mistakes in spelling and punctuation were corrected and one or two changes in word-order were made to make the writing sound more natural.

The third stage was to try to make the general argument clearer by giving each paragraph a title. That might have been a mistake; originally, the introduction was a piece of continuous prose and it seemed to be taking shape quite nicely like that, but in the end the writer thought the sub-headings would help the reader get into the book more easily. He may have been wrong, and still isn't quite sure, but . . . decisions have to be made at some point or you will never stop tampering with your writing. Good advice can sometimes be: 'Now leave it alone!'

The last stage was to read it aloud. It didn't sound too bad, but there were still one or two points to polish, a word to change here, a phrase to alter there. There was another typing error which had been missed. Then it seemed to have reached the stage where there was no more to say, so the page you're reading now was started.

The writer considered whether 'the writer' and 'the reader' could have been better expressed as 'I' and 'you' but decided that, in the context of a book about writing, it was probably better to use the first two terms as another reminder to the reader of what the book was all about.

In ways like that, this page went through just the same process as the others.

Preparing to write

———◇———

The previous section of this book was about attitudes. This one is about making preparations, because a lot must happen before you can start writing confidently and successfully.

Some people sit with a pen and the writing 'just comes'. They say that, if you look at a blank piece of paper for long enough, something will eventually arrive in your head and, almost automatically, the writing will begin to appear. There was a time when this was known as 'waiting for the Muse' – a belief in which the writer claimed that a spiritual presence was doing all the hard work while he just sat there with a quill pen, writing it all down, a kind of humble secretary translating spiritual messages to the earthly page.

Whether or not you believe in such disembodied inspiration, the fact is that a lot of writers do find the sight of a piece of paper nags and nags them until, sooner or later, the mental emptiness is filled and the page has become covered with words.

Other people – especially when they have to write assignments as part of a course of study – need to prepare more thoroughly.

This preparation can take several forms, some of which are encouraged at college by virtue of the fact that they are built into your course – to its timetable, and to the place itself. The fact that there is a Library suggests that you will need to do some reading; the fact that there are sessions on your timetable called 'lectures', 'seminars', etc suggests that you will have to listen and talk as well as read and write.

You may be surprised, in a book about writing, to find a chapter on talking. However, talking about the topic on which you will soon be writing is a vitally important part of learning what you know and think. In many courses, you will find that 'talking time' is organised around sessions usually called seminars. In them, you can begin to put together the knowledge and ideas which will eventually be written down. You can also risk opinions, matching your thoughts against those of others who are learning too, and helped by the lecturer who will try to guide discussion in a constructive way. Even if you don't have seminars, you should still try to find opportunities to talk to other students on your course. Although writing itself can be a solitary occupation, the preparations for it are often spent in company.

Also important to writing is listening – not just to others in your group, but to your lecturer in those rather formal parts of a course known as lectures. There is a difference, though, between listening and simply hearing. *Active* listening in a lecture is itself a skill and can play a vital role in preparing to write.

As you start to collect the knowledge and ideas which come from reading, talking and listening, you will need some way of recording them and organising them into a useful form. Few people can go straight to the final draft of a piece of writing without an interim stage in which they make notes. Note-making is a skill, the stepping-stone from speech, or the written words of others, to a first draft of your own. That is why this section also deals with some effective ways of making notes.

Of major importance in good writing is a sure sense of who you are writing *for*. Good writers manage to sense the needs and expectations of their readers. In college, you will be writing for a very particular kind of reader, someone who will be not only reading your writing but also assessing (and even grading) it. Therefore, it will pay you to consider this reader very carefully. 'Who are you writing for?' offers you some clues.

Once you have discussed the topic and done the necessary reading, collected together your notes and made some sense of them, considered the needs of your reader and how you will try to meet them, the time comes to begin writing. This stage needs careful preparation too, and the final chapter in this section, 'Starting, Planning and Finishing', suggests how to get started and how to plan.

And how to finish, because – as you will see – sometimes the best place to begin a piece of writing is at the end.

Talking

When people are very young and without inhibitions, they talk all the time. Very young children even talk to themselves if there's no one else around to join in. You can watch them playing with their toys and giving themselves a running commentary, often with different voices for the different characters in the game. Those who have studied the early talk of children conclude that they learn two things at least by doing so: the language itself, and all the many things they need to know about the world and their place within it. They are talking their way to a sense of themselves. As they talk, they learn.

It's the same throughout life. We need to 'talk something through' before we can really know a thing, feel secure with it, and understand what we think about it. Even the kind of informal, joking, gossip-talk which goes on in clubs and pubs and over garden fences helps us to rehearse the events of our lives and to know our own position. Without talking, the principal social activity of humankind, we could not learn.

It follows, then, that the right kind of talking will help people to write better. Preparing to write assignments in college will be helped by periods of constructive talk, and you are likely to find that parts of your course have been set aside for this kind of activity.

It depends on the course and the college just what sort of talking activity you will be asked to do. Think of talking in college as a continuum, from the hesitant, hands-up question at the end of a formal lecture to the informal conversation over a drink, and you can see the range of possibilities. In many colleges, three kinds of talking are formally recognised and appear as such on the timetable: **lectures**, **seminars** and **tutorials**.

Lectures

This is an unusual kind of talking because it is normally only the lecturer who speaks. Apart from preachers giving sermons, newsreaders reading the news and poets reciting poetry, you don't often find situations in which one person talks while all the rest listen. Whether or not you can join in with the talking in lectures will depend on the lecturer. Some will tell you that interruptions are quite in order. Wait for the invitation, though, because otherwise interruptions can be disconcerting in a formal lecture. Some will tell you that they will take questions at the end. Some will prefer no talking at all: they talk, you listen. You also make notes, and these can be used in preparing your writing: listening leading to writing.

Seminars

These take the form of a structured discussion on a pre-arranged topic, perhaps after some preparatory reading or after a lecture. A typical seminar group will consist of a lecturer and around a dozen students. Often, a student will have been asked to prepare a seminar paper which he or she will deliver to start discussion: writing leading to talking and possibly back again to more considered writing later on.

Tutorials

These are discussions between the lecturer and a very small group of students – or even one student individually. It is often only in the tutorial that you will have the chance to discuss your writing directly with the person who has read and assessed it. Some colleges build the tutorial into the teaching system as a regular contact between teacher and student; others leave it to the student to contact the lecturer if and when such a meeting would be appropriate. Such contact often occurs after you have received your writing back from the lecturer, who will suggest that, if you want to talk further about it, you should make an arrangement to do so: writing leading to talking again. Other lecturers may be a little more peremptory about it, the invitation coming more in the form of a demand to 'See me!' or even 'See me at once!!' written on the bottom of your assignment in red, impatient, felt-tip pen.

Talking occurs in all these situations, sometimes in a limited way (the lecture), often in a much more participatory and shared way (the seminar) and sometimes in the intensive, thorough way common in tutorials.

However, talking can pose problems for some people, and you may be one of them. While some people feel easy talking in any situation, the more formal contexts found in college can sometimes lead others to become tongue-tied with embarrassment. Their reaction is to say as little as possible. This is not the best policy if talking really does help people to learn.

There are two kinds of talking which you should think about in the context of a course of study: the talking you know in advance you will have to do, and the talking which just happens as part of discussion. One you can prepare for; the other may catch you unawares.

Prepared talking

The commonest kind of prepared talking you are likely to have to undertake in college will come in the form of a *seminar paper*. Your lecturer may decide to organise a series of seminars by requiring each member of the group to prepare in advance a lead-off paper in which the topic is introduced and the main lines of argument established. If so, then your turn will surely come. For a time, you will be in charge of that discussion.

Some people decide to tackle this task by reading an essay aloud to the rest of the group. Indeed, this may be what your lecturer asks for. In this case, you should look elsewhere in this book for all the guidance that is given there on writing essays. Talking is merely incidental to such a reading and much of the present chapter does not, therefore, apply.

However, you should bear in mind that it is often hard to listen with attention to someone reading aloud the kind of writing which is meant to be read silently. There are likely to be differences of style which make concentration difficult. For instance, the use of technical vocabulary, even the structure of sentences, may differ between spoken and written language (in the same way that conversational language would seem quite out of place on the printed page).

Furthermore, there is a *social* consideration to be kept in mind if you are thinking of reading your words aloud. Concentration and understanding in the listener is helped a great deal by the physical behaviour of the person talking. The movement of their body as they talk, the way they use their hands, in particular their eyes, are vitally important in gaining and holding attention, and none of these things comes as naturally in reading aloud as it does in direct speech to a group of listeners.

Reading aloud is a skilled activity. Listen to an actor reading on radio or television. Two things are especially important: *look at your audience* as much as you can, since nothing saps their attention more than watching the top of someone's head as they bury their nose in the text; and *vary your voice*, since a dull monotone quickly induces unconsciousness in the listener. (It has even been known to achieve much the same effect in the reader.) Unless you feel confident that you can use your voice, your body, your eyes and your personality to *animate* the text you are reading so that it sounds more like talking than read-aloud writing, then it is probably better to prepare your seminar paper in a way which will be more appropriate to its setting: people gathered in order to discuss the topic concerned together.

Giving a seminar paper

Good seminar papers share the qualities of clarity and naturalness of presentation. They are given by people who know their paper well enough beforehand to be able to speak *from* it rather than read it aloud. They will also, of course, be familiar with the material about which it is written, so that they can talk interestingly about the topic with their writing as background rather than foreground. They may, of course, refer to their notes from time to time; they may have prepared a written handout for the group; they may well have brought along written extracts and quotations, ready to be read aloud in order to illustrate their talk; but the seminar paper itself is likely to be talk supported by writing rather than writing translated into talk.

Some people never risk giving such a performance without having every word they intend to say already written out in advance. (Many apparently natural and spontaneous lectures are very carefully scripted.) However, such papers are delivered largely from memory.

Other people are happy to talk more loosely and risk all the 'ums' and 'ers' and 'hang-on-I've-lost-my-places' that this entails. That's all right too, and you should not feel embarrassed at not giving a polished performance in which you come to the seminar word-perfect. As long as you have carefully prepared what it is you want to express to the group, have the facts and ideas in your head – and in notes nearby – then remember that, with the probable exception of the lecturer, you will know and understand more about the topic than anyone else in the room. At least for the time it takes to give your paper, you are likely to be the expert.

How you decide to support your spoken presentation with writing is, of course, up to you. You may be confident enough simply to bring notes – memory-joggers to remind you of what you have said and what you will say next. Some people find it helpful to have each main point on a separate numbered index card (the kind you can store in a box in alphabetical order), with any subsidiary points written beneath or on the reverse of each card. Their paper is given by working from top to bottom of the pile of cards. Others will want the whole script written out in full, if only to have it nearby. Even the most experienced lecturers have been glad of the feeling of security this gives them.

It will be wise, though, to check with your lecturer beforehand if the paper is to be collected after the seminar, possibly for assessment. If that is the case, then you will obviously have to prepare your writing in a fuller way. A lecturer may find it difficult to be fair to you if he or she has nothing more to mark than a piece of scrap-paper covered in scribbled notes.

Talk you weren't expecting

This is what 'talking' really means. Talking, in this second sense, is the raw material of your writing. The more constructively you have contributed to discussion, the more likely you are to feel confident when you later come to write. You should be prepared to ask questions, offer opinions, give information – and to say 'I don't know' if that is the case. There is nothing at all wrong with knowing what you still have to work out in your mind, and so nothing wrong in expressing the fact to those who are learning with you.

However, this is more easily said than done. While some people do not mind being the centre of attention, and a few actively seek to be, you may feel embarrassed and try to avoid the eye of the lecturer in case he or she asks you for your opinion, forcing you out into the open. You may even be one of those who practises a look of thoughtful concentration as everyone else speaks round you, indicating in this way that, though reserving your own particular judgment, you are nonetheless completely absorbed by everyone else's ideas and are full of sensible ones yourself – given time. This could be a useful defence, but you need to ask yourself: 'What am I actually defending myself against?'

When you talk in this unprepared way, the first thing to remember is to keep trying, whatever happens. While it is certainly a good idea not to blurt out anything just for the sake of speaking, remaining forever silent is not fair on the rest of the group, and it certainly isn't fair to you. By staying silent, you are cheating yourself of the opportunity to find out what you think, and what others think of that. So don't worry about breaking the silence.

Your lecturer is there to help make sure that everyone has a chance to express their views. However, he or she will need your help in doing so. Discussion is at least a two-way, usually a multi-way, process involving not only two of you but all the others in the group, to whom you should listen when they speak, and who should be listening to you when it's your turn. Listening is the raw material of your talking, just as talking and reading are the basic ingredients of your writing.

Some common anxieties

'What if I get it wrong?'

First of all, there are many occasions when there *is* no 'right' or 'wrong' answer. College is not the same as school. Remember that the questions asked at school are often 'fact' questions in

21

which there is a correct reply. You probably have memories of answering such questions and feeling foolish when the correct answer was announced. However, in the later stages of a person's education, this kind of question is less common and the ones asked are much more likely to be those of opinion or process, questions with no clearly-definable 'right' or 'wrong' answers. Because, at college, you are expected to do much of your learning on your own, it is assumed that you come to a discussion already in possession of the facts concerning the issue. The point of a discussion is not to check on your basic knowledge, then, but to give you an opportunity to develop what you know in debate with others.

Of course, you may still be on the wrong track in answering such questions of opinion or process. In this sense you may be said to 'get it wrong' from time to time. Less so as you get hold of your course but, as you branch out into areas that are new to you, the opportunities for getting it wrong will multiply. A lecturer's 'No, I don't think so . . .' may be words that strike a chill into your soul. Good advice in such cases can be: 'Don't take it personally.' The lecturer is probably more concerned with the general progress of the discussion than with the particular contribution of any one person. Nobody likes getting it wrong, but if you try out something of which you are not yet sure, you are bound to run that risk. This should not stop you from trying; you will still be learning something by the elimination of error and the abandonment of unprofitable lines of enquiry.

'What if I can't make myself clear?'

Try. Your lecturer will help you, and together you may make sense. It does not matter if you don't altogether succeed because, in trying, you are still learning things. Sometimes, a seminar might begin with a general free-for-all in which people get things started by offering ideas on the topic without much, if any, careful prior thinking. This is called 'brainstorming' – a technique in which a group of people begin to gather ideas and solve problems by saying the first things which come into their heads and then sifting out all but the useful ones. Brainstorming is a way of taking risks with your talk, trying out new ideas, seeing what's there in the mind. It's an extreme form of what happens less clamorously in good seminar talking, in which people are always prepared to risk their ideas and opinions for the sake of the general discussion. If nothing comes of your contribution in terms of ideas which can then be taken further by the group, you will still have learned a great deal by knowing what doesn't, after all, add to the group's growing understanding.

'What will the others think?'

This will depend on who the others are: their personalities and their abilities. Some people will say that they resent or look down upon people who speak up in class. You may yourself think it is showing off or an attempt to be ingratiating with the lecturer. (You may even suspect this about yourself.) Generally, however, speaking up is neither of these things. Rather, it is the principal way in which you will learn. It is also the main way in which others will learn, through listening to the talk they may deride in public.

'What will the lecturer think?'

If a lecturer has asked a question, he or she is usually hoping for a response. If it is too difficult a question, say so. The lecturer will rephrase it. In fact, suggesting that a question is too complex, or that you don't know the answer, can sometimes be the most sensible and considered response. Some lecturers are not very good at putting the right question in the best way, and they need help in discovering this for themselves.

In the same way that you need to consider your lecturer's needs as the reader of your writing, so too in discussion you should think of his or her needs as the chairperson of the group. Next time you participate in such a meeting, note the number of times the lecturer invites people to make a response by saying things like: 'What do *you* think? . . . Do you agree with that? . . . Are you sure that's the best way to put it? . . . I'm not sure everyone would take that view.' These and other conversational devices are important techniques for trying to get a constructive discussion under way.

Then there is the range of body movements and – particularly – eye-contact which can invite someone in, or thank someone for their contribution. Imagine, then, how difficult it is for the lecturer whose invitations are constantly declined by members of the group. If you were trying to help someone feel able to make a contribution – by looking at them questioningly, by making a general point while looking in their direction, perhaps even by asking them directly for their views – and if, at every stage, you found the person looking away, or declining your invitation, you would look for someone more responsive. It would be a natural form of self-defence, since many lecturers can think such a lack of interest may be as a result of something which *they* are doing wrong. Try not to let this happen in your case. You will be helping your lecturer as well as yourself if you try to join in.

Final points

Speak up. Ask. Do not let the moment slip by. If you are overcome by shyness, approach your lecturer informally after the session. He or she generally wants to know, will listen, and will help. You are not being bothersome when you do this; people are far more bothered to learn later that your unimpressive written assignment was the result of your not having understood and not having asked when you had the chance to do so in discussion.

Remember that a major reason for talking in the context of a course of study is to prepare you for the task of writing. By risking your opinions in front of others, you are learning to know how strongly they are held, how valid your reasoning, how powerful your case. Furthermore, by listening to others, you are strengthening the organisation of your own thoughts, placing them within the broader context of the thoughts of others, adding to them and taking from them the parts that do not matter after all or those which, in the light of discussion, you have reconsidered. What better way to prepare your mind for the more deliberate acts of writing which will follow?

For talking does not commit you in the same way that writing does. (As the film mogul Sam Goldwyn is reputed to have said: 'A verbal contract ain't worth the paper it's written on!') Talking is more flexible, more open to revision, less formally ordered. It is experimental and can be hesitant, self-doubting . . . as indeed you may feel you are being when you talk in this context. However inarticulate you may think you are being, though, you will always be giving yourself and your lecturer *something* to work on if you open your mouth to speak.

Keep it shut and you will remain a mystery to others – and to a certain extent to yourself.

Making notes

———◆———

To write well, you must have something to write about, so your preparations must include collecting together facts and ideas and storing them in ways which will be useful to you later. Making notes is the most useful way of making these preparations.

There are usually three sources for such ideas: the lectures you attend; your reading; and the sudden idea which comes to you out of nowhere and which, unless you quickly capture it on the back of an envelope, will be lost for good. This chapter deals with making notes on the first two sources of ideas; the third you can handle for yourself, assuming you make a habit of carrying a pen and something to write on.

Making notes is more than simply the recording and storing of information. It is an important part of the process of preparing the final written draft of your assignment: a process in which you not only collect together the raw material but start to give it shape and direction. *Taking* notes is a relatively passive process of recording information which might otherwise be forgotten; *making* notes, however, is a more constructive process in which you think as you record. Aim for skill in the latter because it will help you to learn and also, as a consequence, to write better.

There are some common pitfalls which can make your notes inefficient and purposeless:

- copying chunks of text from books;
- writing out long lists of quotations which may (but just as well may not) be useful later on;

- the frantic, illegible race to capture every word said by the lecturer.

All these are time-wasting activities, though it is easy to persuade yourself that you are working hard as you do them. If you have done these things, ask yourself whether they might simply be delaying tactics, a way of putting off the hard business of *thinking* while at the same time looking busy. Your material has to be worked on sooner or later, so why not start straight away?

Before you embark on any form of note-making, consider carefully the purpose of your notes, and even question their necessity. If, as a result of these questions, you decide that to make notes is going to help you write your assignment more effectively, you will already have a set of questions in your mind, an agenda of tasks to be done, with which the making of notes can help you.

Making notes from lectures

First, consider the *kinds* of lecture you may attend during your course. Lectures vary in function depending on the course you are taking. In some subjects, their purpose is to ensure that all students have the same basic knowledge from which to start their studies. Often, these lectures are arranged as a *course* in which it is important that students are regular attenders, one lecture leading on from the last and onto the next. Miss one and you miss an important element of the whole course. It is likely that the kind of notes made in these lectures will need to be accurate, properly sequenced and effective in prompting your memory in later study. In many ways, they will become the blueprint for much of your later work.

Other lectures are designed to act as 'keynotes' – statements on the subject concerned which will outline some major directions of enquiry, establish some ground-rules for later work, but then leave it to the students to work on their own. Especially in lectures of this kind, the lecturer can often try to be provocative, offering a set of ideas and opinions which are calculated to make you think for yourself – and perhaps disagree. Lectures like this should not be considered as the final word on the subject and so the notes you make may turn out to be shorter than those made in a *course* of lectures.

Perhaps all you need to record are some of the major ideas, marked with symbols like '?' or '!' to remind you of your own position as you first heard them, and to signal to you the possibility of later exploring your response more fully.

A few lectures, often given by visiting speakers, are put into a course almost as a theatrical device: a way of bringing some acknowledged expert into contact with the students so that they can be stimulated by the thoughts of 'a big name'. You may find that making notes in lectures like these is not really necessary. Better to sit and listen and soak up the drama of the event.

In every case, however, the function of a lecture is likely not to be an end in itself but to give you something to work *from* as you study the subject on your own. If that study leads to a written assignment, remember that few lecturers will be likely to receive with much enthusiasm writing which is no more than a restatement of their own words. They will certainly want to know that you have incorporated the ideas in the lecture into your own thinking, and they will expect to see how your reading has helped you as well. Their main interest, however, will be to see how much you have been able to bring your *own* perceptions to bear upon these starting-points to your writing.

Using the lecture

It is a good idea to prepare yourself for a lecture by deciding what it is you want to gain from it. If not earlier in the week, this can be done in the moments just before it begins. You will probably know the broad topic to be lectured on and possibly even the lecture title. With this in mind, you can ask yourself questions like: 'What are likely to be its main concerns?', 'What do I already know on this subject?', 'What further do I need to know about it?', and so on, so that you are in a positive, receptive, questioning state of mind by the time the lecture starts. If you can establish such an attitude from the outset, you are more likely to *make* notes rather than passively *take* them.

Using the lecturer

Strange as it may seem, the lecturer is present in the lecture room primarily for *your* benefit. Too many students attend lectures only because it is required of them to do so. They sit through the lecture with varying degrees of involvement and leave having learned very little. So you should ask questions about a lecturer's methods as well as about what he or she is saying. Sometimes, these methods give you clues about a particular approach to the subject which may be useful to you when you come to write.

Lecturers work in different ways. Some see the occasion as one in which they alone do the talking; others work through interchanges with their audience. Some use a question-and-answer technique as their means of delivery; others leave questions from the class until the end. Some lecturers work from carefully-prepared notes, even to the extent of reading their lectures word-for-word. Others deliver their lecture almost as if they are thinking it up as they go along. (One 'big occasion' lecture on Ancient Greece was delivered faultlessly by a major international expert. His only 'notes' consisted of an index card on which were written the two words 'Ancient Greece'.)

Many lecturers use no more than their own voices in their lecture. Others will add the technology of the lecture room: black- or white-boards, overhead projectors, slide displays, video, scientific apparatus, the lecture becoming more like a demonstration. Many lecturers work with handouts; these can be valuable and should be stored for later reference. Some handouts offer material, perhaps in the form of documentary evidence, which the lecturer will work with during the lecture itself; other handouts are designed for different purposes – perhaps to give reading-lists or even assignment titles. In either case, keep these and read them afterwards.

Select and record

Once the lecture has begun, there are two main considerations to be taken into account: what is and is not relevant to the questions you have already asked before the lecture began; and how the relevant points can be recorded in such a way that they continue to make sense after the lecture has finished. These two considerations both suggest that you will need to be *selective*. Furthermore, the nature of any lecture means that you must take these selective decisions quickly as well as record them efficiently.

There are times when decisions about relevance can be difficult to make, particularly if the lecture seems disorganised or even partly incomprehensible. Try to persevere, however, for what at first may seem to be a disconnected argument may make good sense to you later. If, after reasonable persistence, this doesn't happen, suspect the lecturer and not your note-making ability.

In particular, *listen* for clues in the lecture itself about the structure of what is being said. These can help you organise your notes into related sections. Many good lecturers will help their students considerably by 'framing' their lecture at the beginning and the end with clear signposts:

- To start with, I'll be talking about A. I'll then go on to make three points about B. This will in turn pose certain important questions about C and D. I'll finish with a brief comment on E.

and, at the end:

- What we have been considering today has been X. We have looked at the evidence concerning A, B and C. We have rejected as irrelevant the points made in D, E and F and we have also looked briefly at G. When you think about this for your written assignment, it will help you to keep in mind Y and Z.

There are also important clues to be gained as the lecture moves through its stages: 'hinge-points' which indicate a change of direction:

- Having seen what happens with X, we can now go on and look at Y before examining Z.

a set of subsidiary ideas:

- I've been talking about A but we shouldn't forget to consider the following related points (a, b and c) . . .

a collecting-up of the main points so far:

- Let's stand back for a moment and see where we have got to at this stage . . .

and the point at which the lecturer starts to sum up:

- Before I finish, I will make three more points . . .

Be ready for these indicators of direction and shape. Find ways to record them in your notes, for they help to give you the *structure* of the lecture: as important as the content itself. Furthermore, learn from them how you yourself can frame and structure your own writing afterwards. (More is suggested on 'signposting' your own writing in a later chapter.)

As for the effectiveness with which you record your notes, it stands to reason that the less you write, the less time it will take to get it onto the page and the quicker you will be able to make sense of it afterwards. This means that what you write must count. Aim for the most with the least – the 'Ancient Greece' effect.

Two common note-making systems are used by many people.

- The **linear** or **logical outline** system (see p. 32)
- The **pattern** or **spider plan** system (see p. 33)

On the following pages the same lecture has been recorded using both systems. Notice the way the notes have begun: with a clear labelling of the course, the lecturer's name, and the date. You may not think this very important, but when – perhaps three or four years later – you come to revise your notes for final examinations, it can be invaluable to have your work recorded in this way.

The linear or logical outline system

This is a relatively familiar system of note-making whereby you listen for main and sub-headings and record them, as they occur, in a linear way

Notice the comments in brackets. These are included to show how your notes may be made actively and critically from the outset. This in turn enables you to focus some of your reading on the subject after the lecture and may even give you some directions on how your written work might proceed. A thoughtful and questioning attitude to the topic at this first stage helps to ensure that any follow-up study will have a purpose and be, to some extent, dictated by the lines of thought established here.

The linear or logical outline system

1. PERSONAL, SOCIAL AND EMOTIONAL GAINS

1.1. EMOTIONAL/PERSONAL
- 1.1.1. Extension of emotional
- 1.1.2. Consolidation   "   "
- 1.1.3. Ordering   "   "

1.2. PERSONAL/SOCIAL
- 1.2.1 Extending Experiences
- 1.2.2 Knowledge of others – empathy, sympathy, antipathy.↱ (INTERDEPENDENT?)

1.3. IMAGINATION
- 1.3.1 'mental' imagery
- 1.3.2 Spectator role – active imaginatively.
- 1.3.3 Fantasy game

1.4. ENJOYMENT
- 1.4.1. Release from 'here and now'   (HARDING'S ARGUMENTS AGAINST THIS?)
- 1.4.2 Humour
- 1.4.3 Etc. etc. etc.

2. LEARNING GAINS

2.1 CONCENTRATION AND LISTENING   (PROOF OF THIS?)

2.2 CULTURAL/SOCIAL VALUES
- 2.2.1 race, gender, class
- 2.2.2 multi-cultural issues
- 2.2.3 values and change within a society

2.3 'NATURAL' MEANS OF LEARNING
- 2.3.1 Story and the young child
- 2.3.2 Centrality of Narrative
- 2.3.3 Aid to concept development

3. LANGUAGE GAINS

3.1 EXTENDING LANGUAGE POTENTIAL OF INDIVIDUAL
- 3.1.1 Vocab, Syntax, etc in context
- 3.1.2 Literary/Creative Language

3.2 DEVELOPING CRITICAL AWARENESS
- 3.2.1 Bias, persuasion in text   (SEE RELATIONSHIP WITH 2.2)
- 3.2.2 Literary criticism
- 3.2.3 Literary conventions

3.3 LEARNING TO READ
- 3.3.1 Bridge between written and spoken language (CONFLICT WITH 1.4?)
- 3.3.2 'Book skills' in context
- 3.3.3 Etc. etc. etc.

The pattern or spider plan system

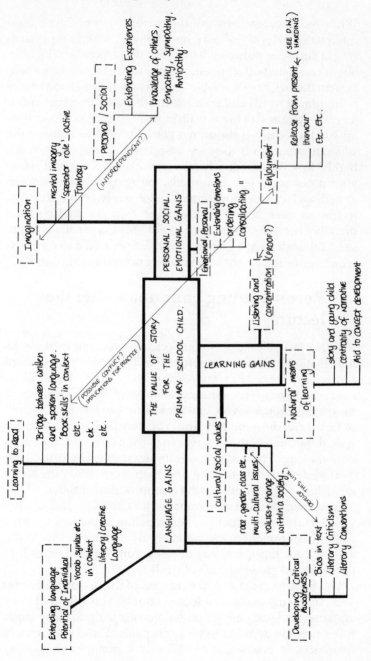

The pattern or spider plan system

While the linear system and the pattern system can be used interchangeably, there may be occasions when one system would suit your purposes better. For those lectures which are about cause-and-effect relationships, for instance, the pattern system is ideal, since it enables you to summarise an idea in the minimum of words and then attach what are sometimes called 'branching notes' to these to fill in more specific points as they arise in the lecture. It also allows you to make links between the separate branches if they are associated in some way. It is a highly flexible system whereby you can develop and refine your notes as the lecture unfolds, for by its nature it is open-ended and can be augmented quite easily, even after the lecture is over. Its main advantage over the linear model probably lies in its visual impact: not only does it allow you to see relationships at a glance; it also acts as an aid to memory, which can be important when making notes for examinations.

Reconstituting your notes after the lecture

To make the fullest use of your lecture notes, and to make the information in them your own, you will probably need to work further on them after the lecture has ended. You will be concerned with reconstituting your notes into a form which makes more sense to you, or with adding more detail as a result of further reading and thinking. You may find as well that this task, done outside the lecture, can in itself be useful practice in note-making. You could, for example, start off by using your own system of note-making and then reconstitute the result into a linear form similar to the examples shown above.

However, the most important use for filling-out and refining your lecture notes comes in their function as preparation for a written assignment or examination. By reading further in the area of your topic, you can develop your original notes into personal and growing units of study.

You have already seen illustrations of the use of brief notes and comments made in a lecture, but as you read and your knowledge of your subject grows, you are likely to make much fuller notes in addition to these originals. These may include references to books and articles and summaries of relevant ideas; personal comments which refer to your opinions about certain points made in the original lecture; and the inclusion of much richer detail, perhaps including relevant quotations.

Making notes work for you in this way not only paves the way for writing your assignments but also provides the basis for a useful set of study units when the time comes for revision and examination.

Making notes from books and articles

Much of what has already been written in this chapter about making notes in lectures will apply equally to making notes from printed materials: they need to be accurate, efficient and purposeful. The two systems described above may equally be used, depending on the type of text you are reading. The main difference – and a positive advantage – between making notes from a text as opposed to a lecture is that you can now work at your own pace: reading closely where necessary, or skimming and scanning over passages, chapters and even whole books if that better suits your purpose.

Gathering information from a variety of sources will probably be an important feature of the first stage of preparing your written assignment. Therefore, it is worth getting to know the system of over-viewing a book since this allows you access to a wider range of information, with the option of discarding the irrelevant and focussing only on what really matters to you, in as short a time as possible.

The purpose of over-viewing a book is twofold: to discover what the book is about; and to find out whether it contains useful information. The *title* should be one of the most important clues about content but, after this, the *contents* page itself is most useful. So look at this and mentally note any chapters that look promising. The *index* can be used in the same way.

- Read the *Introduction*. (If there is one, also read the *Conclusion*.) Once you have determined the general area of the book and located any useful chapters, quickly over-view these by doing the same thing with each one:
  - scan the main sub-headings;
  - look at the illustrations;
  - read the concluding paragraphs.
- See if the book contains summaries of chapters or sections.

It is also important for your future reference to keep accurate records of the books you have looked at, especially if these books are on loan for a limited time. These records should include the *title* of the book, its *author, publisher* and the *date of publication*. A card index is a useful way of storing this information, allowing easy access and retrieval at a later stage. Other details on the card could include specific page references of points you think may contribute to your final written assignment. Here's an example:

> Hall, A: <u>Crimes and Punishments</u>; Robard Press (1984) pages 9–19
> A detailed argument against the re-introduction of capital punishment.
>   Useful footnote references to be followed up.

Later, you could add to this cross-references to other books you come to read on the subject, for instance:

> Compare contrasting argument in:
> Newton, B: <u>Criminal Law</u>; Hillhouse (1979)

If you think the book is likely to be useful, not only for your present written assignment but at later stages in your course, you could also write a short summary of its contents. This need not amount to more than an actual copy of the *Contents* page onto the back of your card.

At some stage, you will also need to read closely to follow a complex argument or process or to assimilate new information. If the text is of a suitable length, and you don't actually own the book itself, it may be a good idea to photocopy the section concerned and make notes and markings directly onto the copy. Precisely how you mark the text or make your notes depends on the type of text you are studying. Obviously, in the case of Literature, where the whole text *is* the content of your course, you will need to possess your own copy so you can scribble your marks everywhere.

'Reading with a pencil', then, is a vital part of preparing to write. The golden rule is never to trust to your short-term memory but to keep careful records of the work you do. Remember that today's reading may be some years distanced in time from that day at the end of your course when you come to take an examination in the subject you have been reading about. By being particularly careful to note down the relevant facts, you will be serving your long-term needs and building the structures and fabric of the writing task which faces you in the much more immediate future.

You will also be practising *precision* in the way you go to work: one of the most important contributions to any successful course of study.

Who are you writing for?

Imagining the reader

No one writes for nobody. Even if you don't expect anyone else to read what you've written, you are writing for yourself. So every piece of writing you write will have at least one reader.

A good way to write badly is to misunderstand or disregard the needs of these readers. One of the most important skills a writer must learn is how to anticipate what the readers want to read and then to provide it.

That does not, of course, mean writing only what you think your reader will *agree* with: your own ideas matter, and it's always possible that your reader may discover something in what you have written which he or she didn't know or hadn't thought about before. What it does mean, however, is finding the right 'voice' on the page for the readers you have in mind. It's a skill you are probably very accomplished in when you speak, being able to match the things you say and the ways you say them to the people you are with and the situations you are in. Think now about spending time doing the same thing with writing.

Talking and writing are different

Think about the differences between *writing* for someone and *talking* to them and you will see major differences between the two ways of making language. When you talk to another person, you can receive feedback in all kinds of ways which tells you whether your message has been received and understood. A nod of the head, a look in the eyes, the saying of phrases like 'I see' or 'I don't understand', even a sequence of small grunts, will tell you instantly how successful you have been in communicating your message and will allow you to modify it as you go along to ensure that it is fully understood by your listener.

This is not the case when you write. Most writing is done in the expectation that it will be read in a different place, at a different time, and seldom with the writer being present. Furthermore, much writing is intended for an audience which the writer has never met: the anonymous stranger with whom the writer may share very little common experience. For example, though I know broadly the kind of person who is likely to read these words – a student in college – I don't know exactly who you are, and so have to make many allowances in what I am trying to express for a wide variety of readers. I must not be too specific or most of you will think I am writing for someone else. And I cannot be too general either, for much the same reason.

Consequently, sending a message in writing can be a much more risky process than doing so in speech. The writer cannot take so much for granted in the reader's knowledge; will have to point things out which in speech would be obvious from the context; must anticipate where the reader may be confused or need more background information; must try to gauge how much the reader knows already. Being too detailed might lead a reader to feel offended ('Does he think I'm ignorant, or something?') while being too general can lead to a reader's feeling lost ('What *is* this person going on about?').

Your lecturer as reader

Of course, the audience you will write for most at college is your lecturer. You are at an advantage here because, unlike the anonymous readership so often addressed in books, you do know that person, if only as the figure you see once a week from the back of a lecture room. In many cases, you can ask a lecturer exactly what he or she requires from your writing before you begin.

However, lecturers can be paradoxical people in their needs as readers. On the one hand, their function is to help you learn.

39

On the other, they are often in the position of assessing the outcome of that learning in the form of your written assignment. So writing for a lecturer is rather specialised and needs to be thought out carefully if it is to succeed.

Put yourself in the place of a lecturer reading something you have written. What kinds of things will he or she hope to find there? It all depends, of course, on what you have been asked to write, but obviously the greater part of the lecturer's requirements will be concerned with its *content*, and in many respects this is not a writing problem at all but rather one of your own knowledge and understanding. (You may like to follow this line of reasoning through and consider the ways in which good writing can emerge from thoughtful reading and from thorough discussion: both ways of finding things out in the first place.)

Read the question

You can learn a lot about your lecturer's needs and expectations from the way the assignment title has been phrased (see 'Starting, Planning and Finishing') and anything which is said about it in addition. Your lecturer may set you a writing assignment with specific conditions, like 'Do not write more than 1500 words' or 'I expect to see how well you have related your reading of X to your understanding of Y' or 'You don't need to go into great detail – just make sure you outline the main stages of the process' and so on. If this is the case, you are already in a much clearer position to provide what is asked for.

On the other hand, you may simply be presented with an essay title ('Discuss the effects of post-war legislation on town planning in the south-west') and be expected to deal with it in any way you can. This is where knowing the needs of your reader can be particularly helpful in writing successfully.

How much should I put in?

When you write for a lecturer, you are undertaking a task at least one feature of which is unique to this kind of writing: in many cases, your reader already knows at least as much as you do about what you are trying to say. This is precisely why you have been asked to write in the first place: to demonstrate that your own knowledge is adequate. This puts you in a difficult situation: you have to decide how much information to include so that your lecturer understands what you are writing about, and how much you need to include just to show that you know your subject. In making a judgment on what to put in and what to leave out, it will help if you err on the side of including too much information rather than too little. If you aren't sure, imagine the lecturer reading your assignment and asking, 'Why on earth hasn't he/she mentioned such-and-such?'

How much should I leave out?

On the other hand, you can take some shared knowledge as agreed between you. If, for example, you are writing about *Hamlet*, you do not need to remind your lecturer that the dramatist, William Shakespeare, 'was an English dramatist writing during the reigns of Elizabeth I and James I', since it will be assumed that this much, at least, can be taken as read in the context of college-level writing about the play. On the other hand, if you write, 'Shakespeare was influenced by other writers when he wrote *Hamlet*' your lecturer may want to be convinced that you know who those other writers were and that you aren't just taking a short-cut to save yourself from having to look up their names.*

A lecturer won't expect you to know everything. You are, after all, writing as part of the learning process, so don't pretend to know things you don't. Students can often try to suggest knowledge they do not really have by writing things like 'Many writers on sociology have said that . . .' or 'It is commonly agreed by historians that . . .' or (the oldest trick in the book) 'Research shows that . . .'. This immediately alerts the lecturer to ask, 'Well, *who* says that?' or, '*Which* research precisely?' and if no answer is forthcoming, he or she will probably assume that you are just trying to impress. In general, it is sensible to let your reader know clearly just how much you do know and that you are aware that there is still more to find out. 'I have been reading so-and-so on such-and-such and she says that . . .' is a more effective way of putting things than the examples above – if only because it's more likely to be true.

Many writing assignments set in college require students to

*If you feel that to mention them would interrupt the flow, put them in a footnote, like this.

select from the possible things they could say only those which are strictly relevant to the question in hand. In this case, putting in too much will suggest to your lecturer that you can't see the wood for the trees. You may be able to judge whether this is the case from the assignment title. If, for example, you are asked to 'Summarise . . .' then putting in everything you know is unlikely to satisfy the needs at least of that particular reader.

The 'educated non-specialist'

Your lecturer is an expert (probably). However, when you write for a lecturer, one way to think of him or her is as that useful figment of the imagination, that helpful 'theory', which is sometimes referred to as 'the educated non-specialist'. Finding out who the educated non-specialist might be is probably best done by asking who he or she is *not* . . .

Writing in an academic context means aiming what you write at a specialised and hence restricted range of readers. At one end of the scale, academics write for each other, often in the form of articles in learned journals. They need not hold themselves back. They can use the language of their subject, comfortable in the knowledge that all their technical vocabulary will be instantly understood by people, like themselves, who are experts. Since no one else is involved, there is no need for them to simplify or to consider a variety of readers' needs. They can leap in at the deep end, confident that those reading what they write will either know as much as they do about the subject, or will be quite at ease in finding out, since they begin from the same place. Introductions and initial statements can be made very quickly: almost as in a conversation where the participants already share all the background knowledge and want to get straight down to details. Such anxieties as these writers may have are not about whether they have made themselves clear or interesting to the outsider, or whether their style is lively, attractive and comprehensible. Rather, they concern questions like: 'Have I covered myself against charges of inaccuracy?', 'Have I remembered to acknowledge my sources thoroughly?', 'Is my argument sound?' The nightmare for such writers is that what they write may be rejected by their peers; after all, their academic reputations are on the line each time they publish.

At the other end of the scale, academic writing can be for newcomers to the subject, and these can be of two kinds: either the new student, someone committed to the subject and who is about to start the long process of becoming expert, or the interested man-or-woman-in-the-street, who has no intention of making a serious study but who would, nonetheless, like to know in simple terms what it has to offer.

Writing directed at the first kind of reader is often used at the outset of college courses: *Introductions to . . .* the subject which, while assuming no prior knowledge, will also expect their readers to be prepared to do some work along the way. Many of these books find a place in college courses as standard introductory textbooks. For the second kind of reader, more likely titles might be *So-and-so made simple,* or *Step-by-step through . . .* a book written by an expert who wants to take readers right from the beginning in a clear, lively and simple way – perhaps to the point where that reader becomes interested enough to want to find out more through a course of study.

Somewhere between these three positions – of the expert, the new student and the interested browser in the bookshop – exists the person known as the *educated non-specialist.* This is a person who is knowledgeable enough not to need everything spelled out in elaborate detail, already knowing something of the area involved and being sufficiently interested to want to find out more. However, the educated non-specialist is not as knowledgeable as the expert, so addressing his or her needs means being careful not to take some knowledge for granted. The background may be known, but the detail needs explicit treatment. The educated non-specialist has no particular axe to grind and is open to new ideas, different interpretations, novel approaches. On the other hand, this reader is no fool and will need evidence and reasoned argument before accepting what you write. Such a reader has an open but acute mind.

It is to the educated non-specialist that much successful college writing is addressed, and it is into this role that many lecturers will try to put themselves as they read and assess your work.

Be clear

Lecturers will want to find evidence that you have understood what the assignment is asking you to do and that you can express your ideas in doing so clearly and directly. Clarity is essential: you will need to help your reader to find clear and reasoned ways through your writing from beginning to end. More advice on how to signal the main directions of your writing is given in the chapter 'Signposts'. Directness of style is easy to demand but sometimes hard to achieve. Finding an appropriate style is often difficult, as practised writers know only too well. For the purposes of writing for your lecturer, the best policy is usually to try to make your language simple, direct and without unnecessary decoration. Once again, some of the problems will be dealt with later in the chapter 'Style'.

Mechanics

One thing all your lecturers will demand is that your writing conforms to the normal habits of written language in terms of spelling and punctuation. Two chapters later deal with problems which writers can confront in these largely mechanical, but no less vital, aspects of written language. They will also expect clarity of presentation. You need not type your work – though it can sometimes create a good impression – but you should be able to write neatly and legibly. If you are lucky enough to have access to a word-processor, you will find that making corrections is very easy – so much so that, unless you're careful, you could go on forever changing what you've written to get it just right. Some word-processors have a spelling-checker. If yours is one, make sure it's not an American version or you may present written assignments with spellings (like 'color') which are correct – but only on the other side of the Atlantic. A later chapter looks in more detail at word-processing.

*

A major step towards better writing, then, is to try to understand the needs of your readers. In college, this is simplified by the fact that they are usually only one in number. However, it is likely that he or she will not only be reading what you write for pleasure or enlightenment but will also be assessing it. To offset this potential setback, remember that, before you put pen to paper, you can often ask this reader to let you know just how to go about providing what is required.

Few writers in other contexts enjoy this privilege.

44

Starting, planning and finishing

---◆---

You have the assignment title and the deadline draws nearer. You've been to a lecture. You've talked through ideas. You've been to the library and done some reading. You've made notes as well. You know the kind of reader you will be writing for. Now what?

Getting comfortable

There's an ordinary human aspect to writing that should not be ignored. It has nothing to do with how much you know about the subject of the assignment, and nothing to do with whether you think you can or cannot write about it. It has everything to do with being physically and emotionally comfortable. People who write for a living – journalists, novelists and so on – have ways of beginning to write and ways of continuing until they've finished. These methods may be more or less formal, but such routines presumably make them comfortable and help them to get the day's work done. So think about your own routines as well. Make yourself comfortable.

The place

Many would suggest a warm room (but not too warm), well-ventilated, with good natural and artificial light; a desk or table, chair at the right height, and time free from noise and distractions. This makes sense, of course, although some of these things are easier to achieve than others, especially at college.

The background

There are more things to consider too, the more personal, even idiosyncratic features that make all sorts of writing an individual activity. Some people like music while they work, while others feel they cannot write a word unless all is perfectly quiet. Some people are casual about where they write – to the extent of writing in bed or in the bath – while others prefer the formality of a particular desk, a particular view from the window, a particular kind of pencil, sharpened in a particular way.

Rituals

There are also preparation (or substitution) rituals, like putting the cat out at bed-time: pencil-sharpening, tidying the desk of other papers, watering the plants, making yet another cup of coffee. One best-selling author avoids the need for these by always ending a day's work in the middle of a sentence. In this way, on starting up again next morning, he is instantly back into the stream of thought he interrupted the night before. These are all ways of settling oneself to the discipline of writing, or – if they go on too long – of avoiding it.

Rewards

Writing *should* be a disciplined and thoughtful activity when you actually begin, but that is no reason for it to be unpleasant, so give yourself rewards for achievement. Work for an hour or two and then make a drink, go jogging, listen to some music. . . . Give yourself a short break, but make sure that you have done a certain amount of work before your reward and you will find, slowly and surely, that your writing is beginning to take shape.

Other people

So far, this suggests that writing is rather a solitary activity, but this need not be the case. Some students may feel a sense of competition because so much of the writing they do is asses-sed. For this reason, they may want to keep things to them-selves. On the other hand, their solitary writing may stem from a lack of confidence, not wanting to share their ideas with another person for fear of rebuke or ridicule. But it can help to talk through ideas with friends, or to read a draft version aloud. Even if your friends don't listen, you might well discover, on hearing your own voice, that something you have written could have been better expressed. If you feel particularly worried about an assignment, it could help to ask your lecturer for advice. It may be that the title you have been given is not sufficiently explicit and he or she may be able to clarify it for you. If your lecturer is willing, talking through your ideas together may also give you confidence, so that you are better able to commit those ideas to paper.

The process

Writing like this is not a single action, performed and then finished until next time. It is a considered process, achieved slowly over time. So 'taking shape' is an important notion to consider when thinking about writing. Writing is not a linear process where you start at the beginning and go on until you reach the end. A writer should constantly be going backwards and forwards, reading and re-reading, writing and rewriting. In this way, the act of writing is more like modelling a sculpture and less like drawing a straight line.

The modelling process starts with a plan.

Planning indicators

To begin your planning, make sure you understand exactly what you're being asked to do in the assignment. Read the assignment title with care. Then read it again. You may think you know it off by heart, but have you read the *clues* inside it which may help you to get started? Recognising these clues may help you to decide on the kind of assignment you should be planning. Certain words in the title, called *indicators*, can sometimes hint at the structure of your assignment. This structure is important because it is what gives shape and coherence to your ideas. Here are some examples of assign-ment titles and the indicators they contain.

'Discuss the advantages and disadvantages of . . .'

This requires, in the main, a two-part structure. You may discuss the advantages and disadvantages alternately, or you could deal with all the advantages first, followed by the disadvantages (or vice versa), as in the example below. In either case, there should be weighing-up of ideas in the assignment, which is almost certainly going to end with some sort of judgment. The judgment shows that you have actively considered the advantages and disadvantages and have not merely listed them – a danger in this type of assignment.

Example A: Discuss the advantages and disadvantages of modern-dress productions of Shakespeare's plays.

Advantages	Disadvantages
Accessible for present-day audience	False sense of 'period' – incongruous
Simplicity	Alienation of audience (conflict with their expectations)
Relationship of modern staging with text, making meanings clearer	Incongruity of language and staging ('People just don't talk that way these days!')
Chance for new insights into play	
Cheaper to stage (?)	

Judgment:

Depends on play (genre, text; interpretation)

Potential audiences? How will they react?

Balance needed in repertoire between the traditional and the modern/experimental.

'Compare and contrast . . .'

This is a slightly different version of the structure shown above. 'Compare and contrast . . .' may appear to require a two-part structure, but you need to look closely at what you are actually being asked. For instance, if the question asked you to 'Compare and contrast the siting of retail outlets in Britain and the United States', it would not be sufficient to write two separate accounts of trade in the two countries: you would also be expected to show in what ways the pattern of trade is similar and in what ways it differs. Expressed in a diagrammatic plan, the structure may look like this:

Example B: Compare and contrast the siting of retail outlets in Britain and the United States

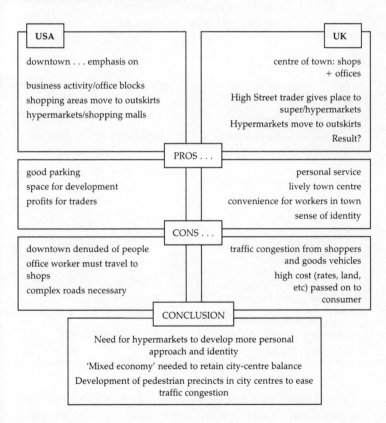

USA	UK
downtown . . . emphasis on business activity/office blocks shopping areas move to outskirts hypermarkets/shopping malls	centre of town: shops + offices High Street trader gives place to super/hypermarkets Hypermarkets move to outskirts Result?

PROS . . .

good parking space for development profits for traders	personal service lively town centre convenience for workers in town sense of identity

CONS . . .

downtown denuded of people office worker must travel to shops complex roads necessary	traffic congestion from shoppers and goods vehicles high cost (rates, land, etc) passed on to consumer

CONCLUSION

Need for hypermarkets to develop more personal approach and identity
'Mixed economy' needed to retain city-centre balance
Development of pedestrian precincts in city centres to ease traffic congestion

'Describe the effects of . . .'

This example deals with outcomes, effects and results, a type of assignment you are likely to come across particularly in history, although this title is taken from geography. The indicator in the example is 'effects'.

Example C: Describe the social and environmental effects of changes in the agricultural industry, referring to any developed country you have studied

```
┌─────────────────────────────────────────────┐
│      CHANGES IN AGRICULTURAL INDUSTRY         │
│                                               │
│   Increasing specialisation and intensity (EEC) │
│     Loss of land (industry, motorways, etc)   │
│     Gain of land (clearance, drainage, etc)   │
└─────────────────────────────────────────────┘

┌──────────────────────┐    ┌──────────────────────┐
│  CHANGES IN LAND USE  │    │  (Bio-) TECHNOLOGICAL │
│     Monocultures      │    │        ADVANCE        │
│  Increase in arable land │  │  Increased mechanisation │
│  Decrease in pastureland │  │     Plant breeding    │
│                       │    │  Increased use of fertilizer │
└──────────────────────┘    └──────────────────────┘

┌──────────────────────┐    ┌──────────────────────┐
│    ENVIRONMENTAL      │    │    SOCIAL EFFECTS:     │
│      EFFECTS:         │    │   Rural de-population  │
│                       │    │  Decline in labour force │
│  Changes in landscape │    │  Fewer farms and farmers │
│  Loss of natural habitats │ │   Fewer family farms  │
│  Clearance of woodland │   │      Bankruptcy       │
│  Draining of marshes, etc │ │                      │
│      Pollution        │    │                       │
└──────────────────────┘    └──────────────────────┘
```

The examples so far have given some clues about the possible structure of an assignment. Other titles may also give clues, but in a less direct way. For example, 'Show how you would develop children's reading in the junior school' suggests that what you will be writing about is a *process*. The indicator is 'develop'. Here's another process example: 'Outline the light and dark stages in photosynthesis'. In this example the indicator is 'stages'. (Sometimes you may actually find the word 'process' in your title, in which case you are off to a good start.) The example below shows a possible structure for a 'process' assignment. The indicator is '. . . the way (in which) . . .'.

Example D: Describe the way in which the concentration of sugar in the blood is regulated.

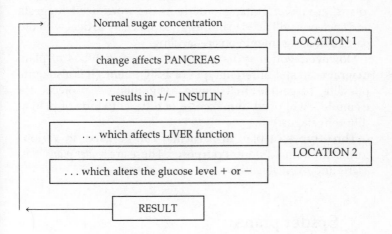

Notice key words in the plan such as 'affects', 'alters'. 'results in', all of which are concerned with change, and which should be borne in mind whatever the subject you are writing about. The references to 'location' are reminders that, in this type of example, details will be required about where such changes take place and the mechanisms involved.

Some titles give little or no clue to structuring at all. 'Write what you know about the legal aid system' leaves you free to write about all kinds of things, organised in any way you choose, but it doesn't give you much support. In such cases you would be well advised to give yourself a structure before you begin to write. You could do this by writing down some sub-headings and these could help you organise your thoughts before you begin a more detailed plan.

Different sorts of plans

It should be clear from the above examples that you should spend some time in careful planning, and that your plan will have to match the kind of assignment you have been given: different plans for different kinds of writing. In particular, you will have seen that it can be the graphic representation of your ideas in plans like these (a 'picture' of your thinking) which can be of most help in preparing to write.

It would make life easier if there was a single agreed selection of plans which you could choose from once you had decided upon the kind of assignment you had to write. However, 'plans' are never quite as orderly as the word itself suggests and each one will need to be designed specially to deal with the particular assignment you are tackling.

However, you may have seen that certain types of plan/ diagram can suit different types of assignment. (It is also quite possible, of course, that longer assignments – projects, for example – will need to make use of different kinds of plan at different stages.)

Three types of plan in particular can be used, in various forms, for many different purposes. These are *spider plans, flow charts* and *tree diagrams*.

Spider plans

These are useful for titles whose indicators suggest outcomes, results and implications. There will be a main event placed in the centre of the diagram (the spider's 'body') and the results extending out from this (the spider's 'legs'). You can even make connections running in circles round the centre (the spider's 'web'). The example on page 33 in the chapter 'Making notes' is similar to this type of plan.

Flow charts

These are suitable plans for titles which ask for descriptions and explanations of processes, or of how something changes from one state to another, or of how one event or action can set up a chain reaction. They are also useful for planning arguments which contain alternative possibilities: 'If X then go this way; otherwise, go that way'. (Flow charts are for the logically-minded.) The last example, on blood sugar, was a kind of flowchart. There's another on page 115 in the chapter 'Paragraphs'.

Tree diagrams

Here's a tree diagram of the chapter you are reading at the moment, up to this paragraph:

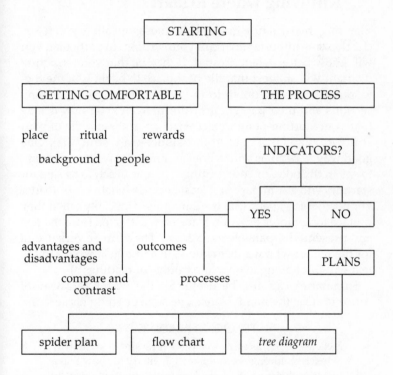

These are very useful indeed, especially for assignments which require categorisation and the establishing of relationships between different parts. Starting with a single 'root' (normally at the top of the page so that, in fact, the whole 'tree' is upside-down), a tree diagram then branches out into its component parts. Each part in turn branches out into its subordinate parts, rather like the branches and twigs on the tree, and so on indefinitely. Alternatively, you could envisage the 'tree' as a 'family tree' with the different parts representing either 'brothers and sisters' (appearing at the same level in the plan) or as 'children' (who appear on the level below). In this way you can plan how different parts of the writing relate to each other vertically and horizontally: some features depending on others higher in the hierarchy of the plan's structure, with others being at the same, horizontal, level.

Knowing where to start

Planning the structure in ways like these will allow you to see clearly some important parts of your writing. In particular, you will know better where to start. It may be that your structure diagram will suggest that the best place to begin is at the top, working your way down to the bottom through succeeding sections and their paragraphs. Alternatively, you may decide that your starting-point in fact turns up in the middle of your structure plan (as it does in the 'spider-plan' structure). One good way to begin is with a brief summary of what you intend to say in the body of your writing. There is much to be said for starting with a summary, not least because it helps your reader know what to expect. (Such summaries, especially when they preface long pieces of writing, are even extracted from the text and presented separately as *abstracts*. They can be very useful for the reader who wants to know, in a nutshell, what's in the text without having to go to the trouble of reading it!)

Summaries can also be useful for the writer as a way of concentrating the mind. Here's one such opening paragraph:

TEACHING READING

I will argue in this essay that there is no single 'right' way to teach children to read. Instead, I will try to show that a sensitive balance of several different methods can be effective. In making this case, I shall look at three teaching approaches in particular: phonics, look-and-say and the whole language approach. I will consider the ideas of several writers who have studied the teaching of reading, concentrating on those of Frank Smith. I will also give some illustrations of various approaches which I used – with varying degrees of success – in my own teaching practice.

54

Finishing

Having an idea about the structure of your writing should also give you some idea about its *ending*. The point at which you finish writing is a kind of goal (as well as a relief). Everything you have been writing up to this point should lead to your concluding statement.

It can make sense, therefore, to give thought to the ending of the assignment first, from there planning how you are going to reach it. You could even try writing the conclusion first of everything, like this:

> It follows, therefore, that there is no single method of helping children learn to read. The illustrations demonstrate that some children seem to learn to read in spite of being exposed to the so-called less successful methods, while others, who have had the type of learning experiences that this essay recommends may still be failing to grasp entirely what reading is about. The nature of learning to read is a more complex matter than simply choosing appropriate reading schemes. Flexibility on the part of the teacher, an understanding of the reading process, and of the needs of the individual child, are crucial factors in helping children to read.

When you have sketched out the last paragraph, like the one above, you should have some idea of what you're going to have to write to arrive at that point, and this should inform your planning. For instance, the example suggests that there will be at least three sections to the essay on teaching children to read: flexible teaching methods; the reading process; the needs of the individual child.

As well as the advantages which writing the last bit first can give you in planning your writing, the ending is a very important part of the written assignment in its own right, and you should give it some thought. As your lecturer comes to the end of your writing, he or she may be thinking about what grade to give you. If your ending gives the impression that you have stopped writing because your writing hand was tired, then you should not be surprised if you find the word 'Conclusion?' written on the bottom. So make sure that your final section rounds off your writing convincingly.

Conclusions

Don't fall into the trap of merely repeating in summary everything you have written; this is not a conclusion. Similarly, your lecturer will not be tricked into thinking that you have written a conclusion just because you have included phrases like 'Therefore we can see that . . .' or, even more obviously, 'In conclusion . . . '. Conclusions must be genuine; a bringing-together of the main ideas you have been writing about in detail through the body of the assignment, and a final statement which your reader can see has been arrived at as a result of the writing you have done throughout.

There are different kinds of conclusion. They may propose solutions to a problem; they may show you making up your mind about an issue; they may suggest further developments; they may draw together the threads of an argument and sum up your own standpoint; all will bring the writing to a neat close.

The example paragraph above concluded an essay which had as its title: 'Outline some approaches to the teaching or reading in the early years and discuss, with reasons, which approach you would adopt for your own class.' Through the body of the essay, the writer discussed different approaches to teaching reading and showed, through examples, that the 'reading scheme' is not the only source of children's reading experiences. The writer's conclusion is . . .

> . . . there is no single method of helping children to read
> . . . and learning to read is a more complex matter than
> simply choosing appropriate reading schemes . . .

The conclusion shows the writer making up her mind about teaching-methods as a result of the argument dealt with in the essay up to that point. It is clear, and above all it has been *achieved* as a result of the whole essay and not simply added to the end for want of a better way to finish.

Is that all?

No. Having written your conclusion, you may think your assignment is finished. However, you should always read through your work at least once, if only to check for mistakes you missed at the time. Better still is to leave it for a couple of days before reading it again. Things which may have sounded obvious when you wrote them may seem less so when you look at them a few days later. Read the assignment aloud, or ask someone else to read it back to you. Does it sound all right? Does it make sense? More importantly, does it answer the question? The assignment may benefit from an extra sentence or two to clarify meaning, the rewriting or rewording of a phrase, the reordering of certain paragraphs for more clarity or emphasis. These may not take long to do, but they will make an important difference – and will also make your reader's task easier.

There are three other points to remember as well.

Have you written your *full* name clearly on the assignment? You may think your lecturer will remember who 'Mark' or 'Liz' is, but there may be others with those names on the course as well. Just in case your writing is mislaid, it is also a good idea to write the name of your lecturer on it too, perhaps with your year group, course name, etc.

Make sure you have written out the full title of the assignment as well, preferably on a cover sheet. This not only helps to create a good impression but also to avoid problems of identification for your lecturer. 'Jude the Obscure essay' is obscure indeed. 'Physics for Dr Evans' isn't much help since Dr Evans has probably been marking physics assignments for most of her professional life.

And finally, hand it in on time. Not only is it business-like to meet agreed deadlines; there are other reasons, too, why handing in work punctually is a worthwhile aim. From the lecturer's point of view, remember that he or she spends many hours each week in assessing written assignments, work which needs to be planned into the schedule. If your work is late, you interrupt someone else's plans – and such discourtesy will not please them. From the students' point of view (and human nature being what it is) there is a further reason why handing work in late meets with general disapproval: if everyone else can manage to meet deadlines, they will not take kindly to those who give themselves another few days, or even weeks, to complete the same piece of work. This is especially true if, as a result of that extra time, their work reaches a higher standard than would otherwise have been possible, so gaining a higher grade. In fact, colleges often operate a system which tries to prevent people gaining an unfair advantage by postponing the moment of submission: perhaps one which allows students a working week after the deadline, but only on the understanding that work handed in during this time can receive no more than a bare 'pass' mark.

As well as the usefulness of deadlines in helping everyone involved, writers and readers, to organise their work within a sensible time-frame, there is also a hidden message which you should bear in mind, referred to by some people as 'the hidden curriculum'. Being a student means being given considerable freedom in organising your work the way *you* decide. However, there is little freedom without responsibility, and people who fail to meet their responsibilities when it comes to submitting work on time are felt by most lecturers to be falling behind in that hidden part of the agenda of any college course.

If for no other reason than personal pride, then, try to submit your writing by the date agreed.

The writing system

◆

This section deals with spelling and punctuation. It also looks at paragraphs and 'signposting' – the ways in which writers can help readers to find their way around the inside of a written text.

People with anxieties about their writing skills usually worry in particular about their spelling and punctuation. If those are faulty, somehow all the other parts of the writing system – to say nothing of the ideas expressed – become part of the background blur. This tends to be true of readers as well: a piece of writing with basic mechanical errors seldom demands the same respect, no matter what it may have to say, as one in which the mechanics are in perfect working order.

This anxiety may be because, as children, the writers became used to having their errors in these two aspects of the writing system regularly pointed out by teachers, with varying degrees of impatience. For many developing writers 'Watch your spelling!' and 'Punctuation! Sentences!' are common – and increasingly depressing – messages throughout the school years. If you were one of those writers, you may have found that they have led to a recurrent anxiety each time you pick up a pen.

Yet as you will see in a moment, your problems with the mechanics of writing are insignificant in comparison with what you have already achieved. You have mastered most, if not all, of the writing system, and though parts may still give you trouble, they should never be allowed to give you nightmares.

The thinking behind this part of the book is simple: you can't eliminate errors if you don't *know* they are errors. So you must

61

develop a habit of mind in which, more perhaps than you have in the past, you observe yourself writing. The idea is not that you become even more self-consciously shy of your own writing than you may already be, but that you stare it in the face. Only that way will you be able to recognise your mechanical problems and put them right.

Neither can you correct errors if you don't know how to. So you will find in this section a description of some of the mechanics of the writing system (in particular, punctuation) as well as ways in which you may be able to understand better how the spelling system works.

Bear in mind that there is a difference between *errors* and *mistakes*. Everyone makes mistakes: slips of the pen, momentary lapses of concentration, the mind leaping ahead of the hand so you leave out letters or even whole words – these are things which happen to all writers. That's one reason why *reading your own writing* is so important: how else will you notice the obvious mistakes you will almost certainly have made in the first draft?

Errors, though, are different. People who make writing errors often *don't know* they do until someone points it out or until they suddenly discover it for themselves. These are the errors of ignorance, and so of innocence. Until you are aware of them, they will remain.

Some errors are errors of desperation. You have probably been told regularly that you are making them, but have never been told how to put them right. What's more, the longer it has gone on, the harder it becomes to ask and a kind of paralysis sets in. It can be embarrassing to acknowledge that you don't know something you feel you should have known for years – even though your writing proves the question to be a necessary one. This section tries to help you find answers to questions you did not like to ask.

Not all errors are innocently-made. You also know when you *think* you may be wrong, for example when you are uncertain of a spelling, or when suddenly you find that word you thought you could spell looks unfamiliar – wrong – on the page. From now on, don't trust to luck: develop a slightly suspicious attitude to your writing whenever you think you may be moving into unknown territory ('Am I *sure* that's correct . . .?') and check to see.

Some errors never appear at all. These are even less innocent.

Writers who suspect they may be about to make an error often retreat to familiar ground instead. For example, most people will admit to the experience of choosing a second-best word because they don't know, or can't remember (or can't be bothered to look up) the spelling of the one they really wanted to use. If you have done this, don't do it again! It's a pity to spoil an otherwise well-expressed idea for want of a moment's research. You should *always* have a dictionary nearby, for spellings as well as meanings, and the book you're reading now should help you with other aspects of the writing system.

So challenge yourself from now on to find out about how the writing system works, and about how your own writing corresponds with that system. If it's a case of spelling errors, spend a little time finding out how you can go to work on your spelling; if you aren't certain of how a particular punctuation mark works, read the chapter 'Punctuation' and then compare what is written there with your own writing. If you have never really understood when to stop one paragraph and start another, read the chapter 'Paragraphs'. If your writing is generally held to be 'disorganised', then the chapter 'Signposts' could be useful to you.

Above all, don't despair! As you read what follows, never forget that you *are* reading. In other words, your ability to handle the writing system receptively is unquestionably very advanced indeed. There is nothing on this page – no symbol, no punctuation mark, no spelling that you are unable to decode and understand. You know why certain words have been printed in *italics*. The mark '?' communicates to you the fact that a question has just been asked (doesn't it?). You understand that the paired symbols 'qu' are to be understood as representing a particular sound in speech. You know that one of them, 'q', is not used without 'u' in English writing, though the other one, 'u', often appears without 'q'. And you can recognise that the symbols 'q' and 'Q' are different representations of the same unit of the writing system. You are confident that the cluster of symbols which looks like 'question' represents in the writing system a familiar word in your vocabulary. The little dot '.' which is to be found at fairly regular intervals on each page does not look to you like a spot of accidental ink; you know instantly to call it a full stop, and that its function is to tell you that one sentence has just ended and another is about to begin.

So your ability to *receive* written-down language – to decode print – is considerable. Sometimes, of course, reading is not easy: perhaps the content of what you are reading is puzzling or conceptually difficult: maybe you will come across a word you have never met before and will need to go to the dictionary or ask someone else what it means. Maybe the act of reading is hard for you because you're tired or bored or uncomfortable or thinking about something more important – or less important. This is not the same, however, as the inability to decode print but a difficulty of quite another kind. If you were unable to decode print, you would never have got to the position of realising that you don't understand it in the first place.

As you start to solve your remaining problems in *producing* written language, remember therefore that all the systems you need are in your head, or you couldn't receive them. If you could see those systems in sharper focus, where at present some of them may seem blurred, then you would find your difficulties dissolving. The aim of this section is to help you achieve that focus.

Spelling

---◆---

Spelling is one of the few areas in language performance where, in a very precise sense, your work is either exactly right or it is wrong. Reading is rarely so exact: we hypothesise, predict, leave sentences unfinished, change direction, skip and scan. Speaking is full of short-cuts to pronunciation, hestitations, pauses, false-starts, repetitions. In fact, speaking which is too precisely 'accurate' makes the speaker sound odd – as if he or she had been to a course of elocution lessons or was 'speaking with a plum in the mouth'. But with spelling, you can't leave words half-finished. You can't give rough approximations. Wrong spelling shows.

Does it matter? As long as the reader can *understand* what is written, should we be troubled by deviations from normal spelling? Can the occasional holiday from rules and regulations really make that much difference to a sensible reader's response? Certainly, in the context of college writing – and more or less everywhere else as well – the answer to questions like these is 'yes'.

Language is a code and it works through a set of agreed conventions. (You can't make up you own personal rules or no-one would understand you.) In speech, the code is full of variations, depending on the context. For example, we tend to pronounce our words more carefully in a formal setting while relaxing our pronunciation when talking to friends and family at home. For this reason, the same word said by the same speaker can often sound quite different, depending on the circumstance in which it is said. Furthermore, we pronounce our language in different ways depending on where we come from. American English doesn't sound the same as British English, and both kinds of English are themselves rich collections of different varieties of the language (called *dialects*) and ways of pronouncing them (called *accents*).

The same is not true of written language. The basic writing code remains constant, no matter what we may use it to express. Apart from the few words which differ in spelling depending on the national variety used – 'colour' (British) and 'color' (American) for example – and a small number of cases in which alternative spellings are equally acceptable – like 'focused' and 'focussed' – the ways words are spelled are shared by all the writers in the language.

Good spelling conforms to the code which everyone else uses. Good spellers, therefore, are people who have come to match in their own spelling this universally-accepted code. At least, they have done so in the majority of cases. Yet there will always be some words which even good spellers can't spell. What's more, there are likely to be other words which they are *unaware* they cannot spell, words which they think conform to the generally-accepted code but which do not. It is often with some surprise and even embarrassment that they discover their spelling of such words to have been right for them but wrong for everyone else. Learning how to spell means gradually acquiring the agreed spellings for the large majority of the words in a person's writing vocabulary. 'Bad' spellers could be defined simply as those who have further to go to achieve this goal. But remember: no one ever reaches it completely.

So if you think your own spelling is not as good as it should be, all is not lost. You should not think that things have gone too far, by now, for progress to be possible for, as we have seen, failure to spell well is not like a creeping, incurable disease. Rather, it is merely a question of the degree to which a person's spelling deviates from the normal conventions. And deviation is, to some extent, true for us all.

As a beginning, try to cultivate a more positive image of yourself as a speller. People who think they are 'bad spellers' tend to live up to that assessment when they write; those who consider themselves to be 'good spellers' stand a much better chance of putting right the faults they have. This chapter cannot teach you good spelling. (The only way that could happen in a book is by listing all the words in the language,

66

properly-spelled, and asking you to learn them.) Instead, what it tries to do is to show you ways in which you can make yourself into a better speller. You can do this by thinking about what 'good' and 'bad' spelling really means; by understanding a little of how spelling works; and by practising certain techniques.

'Bad spellers'

The problem can be that, once you think of yourself as a bad speller, you are in danger of absolving yourself of responsibility for this failing in your writing performance. 'I can't spell' certainly has none of the tragic implications which 'I can't read' would have, but it is still serious. Yet many people who admit to being bad spellers do so in ways which suggest they are not especially worried by the situation. Some people, when they hand in written assignments in college, often do so with a furtive 'Don't take any notice of the spellings!' as if these were an unavoidable and so blameless blemish in an otherwise sound piece of writing, like an embarrassing uncle the family can do little about. Alternatively, they treat their spelling problem as a rather winsome personal trait, like freckles, which is supposed to lend them a certain charm. Or they proclaim it with a self-satisfied boastfulness, as if to announce to the world that they have decided to opt out of this faintly ridiculous system. (Such writers often display the same approach to their handwriting, which tends to the flamboyantly illegible.)

Spelling better than you think

Confidence is the target for accurate spelling. Indeed, as other parts of this book argue, your present ability should never be dismissed: it is testimony to the accomplishment you already have in producing written English. If your spelling is giving you concern, try this exercise: take a piece of your recent writing, one in which spelling errors have been noted by your lecturer, and count up the number of errors. Now subtract from that number all those errors which are repetitions of errors you have already counted (that is, only count each mis-spelled word once). Then count up the total number of words you have written. Now do some maths: work out the proportion of individual errors to the total length of the writing. For example, in a 1000-word essay, containing 9 individual errors, your error percentage is 0.9 per cent. Which means that your writing is 99.1 per cent accurate for spelling. This could be better, certainly; but it isn't quite the disaster you may feel it to be.

Guessing

You might think that spelling is in some ways the reverse process of reading in that it is an *encoding* rather than a *decoding* of written English. They are connected, of course, and if you can read with little trouble you are already able to recognise how words are spelled. However, there is a crucial difference in the processes by which we read and write which prevents our being able to argue that encoding (spelling) is merely the mirror image of decoding (reading).

When we read, we constantly make guesses about the text in front of our eyes. These are very intelligent guesses, all of them aimed at *predicting* what is about to happen. This can save us time: fluent readers can read in silence faster than the speed of normal speech, their eyes smoothly and swiftly moving down across the print, their minds rebuilding the sense of what they read by taking in the general shapes of the words they see, and guessing at the likely meanings in the context. Contrast that with the early efforts of a young child as he or she works out a piece of written language word by word.

Spelling, by contrast, requires equal attention to be given to *all* parts of the word, from beginning to end. An important difference, then, between decoding and encoding written English is that the first tends to be predictive, guessing the whole from the parts; the second, punctilious to detail, concerned for each part which makes up the complete whole.

Prediction in spelling

Yet there are other ways to predict in spelling. For example, we know that certain words have the same root. Such painfully difficult words as 'haemoglobin', 'haemophilia', 'haemorrhoids' have their root in 'haemal' (of the blood); 'medicine' and 'medicinal', which may cause problems with the 's' sound in the middle, can be traced back to 'medical'. Indeed, many of our apparently illogical spellings can be traced to a root or a system which, once known, makes them less arbitrary, more predictable, than we may have suspected.

Here's another example. The rule itself is of no particular importance but it nicely illustrates the point that English spelling is often much more systematic than many people seem to think. Take the words 'ghoulish', 'ghost', 'ghastly' and 'ghetto'. At first sight, it seems strange that the 'g' sound on the beginning of all these words is made with the letters 'gh' when, at the end of 'enough', the same letters spell an 'f' sound. Yet there are several words which also display such a spelling for 'f': 'rough', 'tough', 'cough' and 'trough' for example. There are still others which spell out no sound at all: 'high' 'sigh', 'light', 'through', 'freight', 'weigh'. From these examples, we can begin to work out a spelling rule:

The letters 'gh' always spell the hard 'g' sound when they occur at the *beginning* of words. However, when used else-where in the word, they can either spell the 'f' sound, or have no sound at all.*

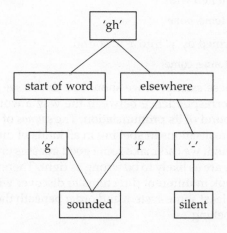

Such rules are called *spelling precedents*. They capture the little patterns which crop up all over the English spelling system, telling us that, although there are bound to be some exceptions (for instance, the word 'aghast' has the letters 'gh' slightly after the very beginning of the word), nonetheless

*For a fuller treatment of this feature of English spelling see Michael Stubbs's *Language & Literacy*, Routledge 1980, p. 51.

there is a tendency which will form the basis for a reasonable prediction.

We learn these precedents in two ways: by reading a lot, and by cultivating a habit of mind which makes us look out for regularities and patterns, a kind of curiosity about the written language which heightens our attention to the way it is made. (There goes another one. Did you spot it?)

Things can become particularly difficult to predict when we have to spell the vowel sounds, and many spelling errors occur in these parts of words. The 'ee' sound, for instance, has several representations in English spelling:

> feel, piece, freak, meter, pique, receive, oedipal

and as for the letter 'o', look at the different ways it can be pronounced; first, on its own:

> cot, woman, women, row, toll, boy, monk, horizon

then combined with other vowels:

> root, book, oats, hoist, hour, louvre, rough, could

and lengthened with 'e'

> pole, tome, bone

or transformed by 'e' into a 'u' sound:

> one, tonne, come

From these examples, we should be able to see that there is no easy correspondence between the way a word is spelled and the sound of its pronunciation. The *sounds* of English will find their realisations in spelling in all kinds of different ways and, although we can make some good guesses on the basis of sound, we are as likely to be wrong as right. Therefore, we will need to look in different directions to discover whether there may be at least some system and order beneath the surfaces of English spelling.

Word structure

From the examples above, we can see that one way to think of the way a word is spelled is on the basis of its *structure*. A word, after all, has parts. Some parts are vowels, others consonants. Each word has a beginning, a middle and an end – and the ways in which the sounds of consonants and vowels can be spelled may vary according to their position in the word. (The 'gh' example is a clear case.) We find parts of the written language which are used in many different words. It's as if much of the spelling of the huge vocabulary of English is achieved by using a comparatively limited stock of spelling-parts, put together in different combinations. The '-ing' endings, for instance, or the '-ation' ending are very common indeed. So are '-ance' and '-ence', '-able' and '-ible', '-er' and '-en'. Certain letter formations habitually repeat themselves in English consonants: 'gh', 'ph', 'th', 'sh', 'ch', 'ck', 'wr'. These are very common pairings, so common that they even have their own name: *digraph*. Of course, each letter can also be used without its pair – except for 'qu', where 'q' is forever isolated unless its roaming partner 'u' returns to join it.

Furthermore, the spelling of one part of the word may affect the pronunciation of another part. For example, one reasonably consistent pattern of English spelling is this:

short vowel + consonant + 'e' = long vowel + consonant

which means that if we find a short vowel followed by a consonant, putting an 'e' after the consonant lengthens the sound of the short vowel, while the 'e' itself remains silent. For instance:

fat (short vowel) . . . fate (long vowel, silent 'e')

Here's another common spelling rule:

long vowel + single consonant/short vowel + double consonant

which means that the long vowel before a consonant is shortened if that consonant is doubled. For example:

tile (long vowel) . . . till (short vowel, doubled consonant)

Predictably, there are exceptions:

tale (long vowel) . . . tall (long vowel)

proving that it would be foolish to trust the rules implicitly.

Probably the best-known of all such spelling rules is the one drilled into us at primary school:

'i' before 'e' except after 'c' when the sound in the word is 'ee'

though once again there are exceptions:

protein, weird, weir, seize, Neil, Sheila, Keith

71

Although, as we have seen, there *are* rules and precedents in English spelling, and though careful study of the English spelling system reveals that it is certainly not the chaotic mess which its detractors make out, it is clearly not the case that we can trust each rule without question. Therefore anyone who thought they would improve their spelling by a careful learning of all the spelling rules they could discover would probably be disappointed: there would always be the interesting exceptions to the rule. Rules are certainly useful; but they shouldn't be relied upon absolutely.

We also know that it would be foolish to place too much reliance in spelling on the *sound* of a word when it is pronounced. If what we wanted was an alphabet in which each written symbol represented unambiguously and exactly just one sound, we would have to use one designed especially for the purpose. The International Phonetic Alphabet consists of a large number of different symbols, each representing one, and only one, sound. For example, it has a great many symbols for all the different vowel sounds made by speakers the world over. Contrast that with the five symbols (a, e, i, o, u) which the English alphabet uses to represent the range of vowel sounds in English. You can see that the English alphabet works in more complex ways, putting letters together to make all kinds of different sounds, either because of a regularity or precedent within the written language, or even because of the way the word first came to be spelled centuries ago. (For example, the use of 'gh' in words like 'ghost' happened because William Caxton, the man who first printed the English language, so releasing it across space and time, mixed up English with Dutch spelling. That was in the fifteenth century, but the habit is still with us.)

What, then, *can* people rely on to make their spelling better? There are two answers: **sight**, and **self-analysis**.

Sight

Poor spellers have frequently been observed to have a short memory span for visual material – and in spelling the visual characteristics of a word are vitally important. Vision, after all, is the preferred sense of human beings. Whereas dogs sniff and bats use sonic echoes, we look and see. So if your spelling needs improvement, consider giving yourself some eye-training. It may sound a little eccentric, but the effects have been dramatic: it has been shown that spelling is improved after visual training in as little as two weeks and, one year later, that significantly higher scores on spelling tests have been recorded in trained over untrained groups of spellers. Furthermore, it is cheap, painless and it avoids the need for long evenings learning rules.

You don't have to train your eyes on spellings alone. Try some games.

- Ask a friend to jumble up some articles on the table (keys, coins, matches, etc). Allow yourself a concentrated look and then, with your eyes shut, ask your friend to remove one of the objects or alter its position. Can you notice exactly what has been changed?
- Look carefully at the pattern on the wallpaper, and then try to draw it from memory.
- Stare hard at the view outside your window and then turn away. How many windows does the house across the road have? Was the front door in the centre of the house, or to the left or right?
- Which side is the badge on the rear of the car you have just been staring at? What did it look like? Could you draw it?

In simple ways like this, you can begin to train your eyes to be more receptive to *patterns* – for spelling is the patterning of groups of letters in highly specialised ways.

Successful spellers tend to use sight and not sound to learn their written vocabulary. You can do the same. There's a simple method – one used in primary schools – and well worth using yourself, because it works. It was developed by the spelling expert Margaret Peters. What you do is:

- **Look** at the word in a book. Try to remember it.
- **Cover** it up so you can't see it.
- **Write** it down from memory.
- **Check** to see if you were right.

The intention to *remember* the word has been made conscious – if only for the time it takes to write it from memory. This is half the battle. (Think of the times you have been introduced to someone, only to forget their name instantly – because you were not at the time making the mental effort to remember it.)

The other way you can best improve your spelling vision is simply by reading as much as you can. People who use printed material regularly (as you will in college) are at a great advantage over those who rarely read. You cannot look at the shapes of written words for long without some of them staying with you. Next time you are uneasy about a spelling, write the word down and then try out all the other possible alternative spellings you can think of. Stare at them all; which one looks right? If your vision is well-trained, you will find it easier to match the correct version to that version of the correctly-spelled word, seen in your reading, which you have stored away in your memory.

And in case you are lost for a spelling as you write, *always* keep a dictionary by you – and use it. Dictionaries are probably used more for checking spellings than they are to discover definitions. If you really want to invest in better spelling, buy a spelling dictionary. On the other hand, a normal dictionary is quite satisfactory for the purpose and will serve the double function of spelling guide and reference book for definitions. If you feel your spelling is weak, make a point of *practising* with the dictionary. Time yourself, if you like, as you look up a selection of words you feel unsure of, working up your speed. Get used to the way a dictionary operates by studying, carefully, the way the words are set out on the page. (Not only will this help you to spell better; it will have the added benefit of extending your vocabulary too!)

Self-analysis

The second method of improving your spelling is to undertake some analysis of where you seem to be going wrong. It's not enough to know that a spelling is 'wrong'; the question to ask is: *how* is it wrong? There are different kinds of spelling error, and if you can get to know the *types* of errors you make, you will be in a much better position to avoid them in the future – not only in the mis-spelled word, but in all other words which are spelled to the same pattern. Self-analysis of these errors is likely to reveal that you are mis-spelling words for different reasons. What follows are some examples of the different kinds of spelling errors that commonly occur. Look at your own spellings and see if any of them appear in your writing.

A.   Words which get confused because they sound like each other

      too to two
      hear here
      feet feat
      there their they're
      through threw
      know no
      weather whether
      won one
      for four fore
      your you're
      paw pour pore
      discrete discreet
      licence license
      practice practise
      current currant
      principle principal
      effect affect
      dependent dependant

All these words are spelled correctly. However, they are often used in the wrong place and so become mis-spellings. In the case of 'licence/license' and 'practice/practise' you may like to learn a useful rule to help you in case of confusion. Pairs of words like these distinguish between the *noun* ('c') and the *verb* ('s'). People get confused because they sound the same, so remember the pair which doesn't

      advice (*noun*) advise (*verb*)

which works in exactly the same way.

B.   Words which have been put together into one (the correct spellings are on the left in bold print)

      at least | atleast
      such as | suchas
      all right | allright (or alright)*
      in spite | inspite
      in front | infront

---

* Alright' is becoming an equally acceptable spelling. This is an example of majority rule: so many people get this spelling wrong (using 'alright') that it is now becoming acceptable. Perhaps in a few more years the 'correct' spelling ('all right') will be thought of as wrong!

C. *Words which have been split in two*

> **instead** | in stead
> **together** | to gether
> **without** | with out
> **already** | all ready
> **although** | all though

D. *Words where pronunciation gets in the way*

> **favourite** | favrit
> **perhaps** | prehaps
> **miniature** | minature
> **ancillary** | ancilliary
> **would have** | would of
> **sentence** | sentance
> **involve** | envolve
> **imaginary** | imaginry
> **attract** | attrac
> **comparison** | conparison
> **input** | imput

E. *Words in which the endings are mis-spelled*

> **appearance** | appearence
> **available** | availiable
> **attendant** | attendent
> **responsible** | responsable
> **formidable** | formidible
> **definitely** | definately
> **applies** | applys
> **existence** | existance
> **independence** | independance
> **dispensable** | dispensible
> **absolutely** | absolutly

F. *Words where the beginnings have been mis-spelled*

> **disappear** | dissappear
> **disappointment** | dissappointment
> **unnecessary** | unecessary

G. *Words with doubled-up letters*

> **beginning** | begining
> **committee** | commitee/comittee
> **getting** | geting
> **written** | writen
> **too** | to
> **innate** | inate
> **accommodated** | accomodated
> **aggression** | agression

H. *Words without doubled-up letters*

> **fulfil** | fulfill
> **fulfilment** | fullfillment
> **commitment** | committment
> **always** | allways

I. *Problems with 'e' and 'ing'*

> **coming** | comeing
> **taking** | takeing
> **using** | useing

J. *More problems with 'e'*

> **department** | departement
> **considering** | considereing
> **excitement** | excitment/exitment
> **precisely** | precisley
> **immediately** | immediatley
> **truly** | truely/truley
> **address** | addresse
> **statement** | statment
> **lovely** | lovley

K. *Words with a missing sound*

> **created** | crated
> **parallel** | parell
> **imbalance** | imblance
> **considered** | consired
> **literature** | litrature
> **interesting** | intresting

L. *Words with letters swapped round*

> **friend** | freind
> **their** | thier
> **strength** | strentgh
> **height** | hieght

M. *Vowel sounds*

> **retrieve** | retreave
> **speech** | speach

N. *Problems with 's' and 'c'*

> **necessary** | nescessary
> **dissociate** | disociate
> **occasion** | ocassion
> **conscious** | concious/consious

You will be able to find other categories as well: spelling mistakes come in all shapes and sizes. Once you begin to recognize the kinds of mistake you make, and the reasons behind them, you will begin to know what you must do to avoid them in the future.

Making a spelling chart

Here's an example of a spelling chart written by one writer with spelling problems. In it, she has written down all the mis-spelled words found in a piece of her writing.

My spelling	Intended word	Letters, etc
there	**their**	ere/eir
comeing	**coming**	e/-ing
alright	**all right**	1 word = 2
preisthood	**priesthood**	ei – ie
useing	**using**	e/-ing
prehaps	**perhaps**	er/re
begining	**beginning**	n/nn
illegable	**illegible**	able/ible
takeing	**taking**	e/-ing
extractsion	**extraction**	tsion/tion

Once she has listed her spelling mistakes in this way, she can find out more about the kinds of mistakes they are.

- In particular, she needs to practise words which lose their 'e' when adding '-ing'. 'Comeing', 'useing' and 'takeing' all show the same error – the most common kind she makes.
- 'There' for 'their' is a carelessness mistake. She knew it was wrong but didn't check.
- She always thought 'all right' was spelt as one word ('alright'), but now she knows it isn't. She should read more. But see footnote on p. 75.
- 'Illegable' shows that she should be suspicious of words which end in '-able' and '-ible'. They are easy to mix up so she must be vigilant when they turn up, and learn them individually.
- She knows from 'preisthood' that long 'ee' sounds can sometimes cause problems because English uses many different ways to spell the sound. She must be careful when words have double vowels.
- 'Begining' breaks a common rule in English spelling: the 'i' sound (as in 'eye') is wrong for the word 'begin'. To make the sound into the same one as in 'tin', the following letter ('n') must be doubled. This rule works for most words.
- Perhaps she pronounces 'perhaps' as 'prehaps'. If so, learning the correct spelling may remind her of the correct pronunciation as well.
- As for 'extractsion', that is another example of a word which she has spelled as she thinks it sounds. She didn't know how to spell this word (and should have used a dictionary to find out) so she guessed instead. It wasn't a bad guess, but now she should never need to guess that word again.

In making this analysis, she can see that the most common problem comes when words must lose their 'e' before an 'ing' ending. So she decides that this will be the first category of spelling error she will attend to. When she feels more confident with that, she will go on to look at other categories of spelling error, gradually working them out of her personal spelling system and replacing them with spellings which belong inside everyone else's.

*

Good spellers are people who *see* rather than *hear* written words. They are aware of the regularities in the spelling system – the precedents and rules – but also know that each one can have exceptions. They spend a lot of time with written language, picking up spellings as they read and so making their task much easier when they come to write. They always read through their writing to check for mistakes. As for errors, they know their limitations: that *nobody* knows how to spell every word in the language. So they use a dictionary to check each time they know, or even suspect, that the spelling is outside their range.

If your own spelling has more errors in it than you feel appropriate for the kind of writing you want to do, then use the ideas in this chapter to help you improve.

Practise *looking* more carefully than you do so that your spelling vision improves.

Remember that mis-spellings happen for many different reasons. So get to know what those reasons are by *analysing* your own spelling errors. Then go to work on your writing, gradually but intently, working on each category of error that you tend to make until you feel you understand it and can make progress within it.

Above all, don't despair! You are a much better speller than you may suspect and the errors still to be corrected are far fewer than the many thousands of written words which give you no trouble at all.

Punctuation

———————◆———————

Punctuation helps us make written language comprehensible. In part, it helps to compensate for the absence from writing of features we use constantly when we talk, features which help to ensure that the words we speak actually express the meanings we intend. These speech features include *stress* (the increased loudness of particular syllables); *intonation* (the way our voices rise and fall melodically to assist communication); *rhythm* and *speed*, even the way we *gesticulate* and use our faces. None of these features is present in writing.

In fact, when compared to speech, writing emerges as a much less complicated and dynamic form of language. Speaking involves the whole body; writing is still. Speaking makes noise; writing is silent. Speaking changes direction (as when the speaker goes back and starts again); writing – English writing at least – can only go from top to bottom, left to right. There are many more sounds in a person's speech than there are letters in his or her written alphabet. So writing has to make its meanings with fewer resources, fewer features in the language code.

The punctuation system, that small group of little black dots and squiggles, can only do so much in helping us to recreate the meaning of a piece of writing, yet without it the written language would be very hard to understand.

Be careful, however, not to think of punctuation as being the visual *equivalents* of these features of the sounds and movements of speech. It would be difficult to think of a punctuation mark which told a reader to 'raise the eyebrows at this point to show doubt' or to 'move your voice down here from a relatively high note to one just below your normal, relaxed voice pitch' or to 'look angry here and say the next syllable in a particularly loud voice while you thump on the table with your left fist'. Punctuation cannot do such things. With one exception (the exclamation mark), all it can do is keep sections of the language apart so they don't get tangled up in each other; or show that a part of the language has been left out; or label a part of the language – to show, for example, that it is spoken by someone else, or that it expresses possession. Important though these functions are, they are not very complicated. Yet people often find them very hard to understand, and so regard punctuation with suspicion and dread. Even writers of quality: the French novelist Victor Hugo is reputed to have sent his publisher the manuscript of a complete novel with no punctuation in it whatever. In a covering letter, he listed all the punctuation marks, with the request that his publisher should 'scatter these through the manuscript as you think fit'.

The punctuation system of English can be fascinating to explore. Some of it is strictly governed by rules which everyone must obey if they are to write correctly; parts of it, however, are open to personal preference. Some of the marks are used a great deal; others only now and again. It is possible to punctuate correctly and adequately using only a handful of marks, and these you should learn. Leave other marks alone unless you are quite sure how to use them.

Unfortunately, the advice given to many pupils in school about punctuation can be confusing because it is only some-times true. Some advice is based on *sound*, borrowing from speech to explain writing. For example, it is said that we will know when to put the full stop at the end of a sentence 'because that is where the pause comes'. But although we do sometimes pause at the end of spoken sentences, we don't always do so. What's more, we pause in other places too. So the 'pause' rule is not really a very reliable one.

Another way punctuation is explained is based on *sense*. An often-used piece of advice is that a full-stop comes at the end of the sentence 'to mark the end of a piece of meaning or sense'. The problem with this is that 'sense' and 'meaning' are not wholly restricted to sentences. A shopping-list, for example, has a meaning – made up from smaller meanings – but would probably contain no sentences at all. At the other end of the scale, one could argue that a book contains a complete meaning, and the sense of the book is not fully expressed until the last of its many thousands of sentences has been written. So the 'sense' rule isn't much help either.

Rather than sound or sense, punctuation is based mainly on language *structure*. If you study punctuation, you will see that the marks serve a structural function; that is, they show how the various grammatical elements of a piece of written language (elements we call 'words', 'phrases', 'clauses' and 'sentences') relate together. Once these relations are made clear, the sense naturally follows – as does the sound when the written language is read aloud. However, you won't need to know much about grammar to follow the explanations below.

> Before reading further, you may like to take a deep breath because we are going to have to use some technical terms any moment now. Don't let them put you off! They mean no harm. They are intended to be helpful. Give them a chance and you'll find that, in the end, they are worth the effort.

The functions of punctuation

Each punctuation mark in the English writing system serves a *function* (some more than one) and it will help you to become more confident in your use of the punctuation system if you think in terms of what each mark *does* in a piece of written language.   The functions of punctuation are:

- to mark boundaries
- to signify attitudes
- to label
- to delete

Here are the major marks, separated into these categories:

Boundary marking	Attitude marking	Labelling	Deleting
full stop comma colon semi-colon brackets dash	exclamation mark	apostrophe question mark inverted commas	apostrophe

You will have noticed that the apostrophe occurs twice in this categorisation. You have a choice here: you can either think of the apostrophe as a single mark used in two different ways, or as two marks, for two separate purposes, but sharing the same name and shape. It doesn't really matter as long as you can use it/them correctly.

You will also find that certain other marks, categorised under one heading, share certain features with another. For example, the question mark (which labels the fact that a sentence has been asking a question) also fulfils the boundary-marking function of a full stop. However, it simplifies description in such cases to make one category predominant.

What follows is an explanation of each category, showing how the marks in that category operate within written language. The explanation, together with the examples, should give you enough information to understand and to work out for yourself exactly how each mark operates. From then on, it's up to you to observe the way punctuation is used in all the writing you read and, of course, to practise it yourself in all that you write.

Boundary-markers

These marks signal the boundary between different parts of the written language. The parts concerned are the sentences, which are marked off from each other by full stops, and the internal parts of sentences (clauses, phrases and single words), which are marked off from each other by commas, colons, semicolons, brackets and dashes.

There are also boundary-markers for parts of written language larger than sentences (paragraphs, for example, or chapters) but these are not, of course, punctuation marks. Instead, we use devices like empty lines, indentations or even new pages: different conventions, though for just the same function of showing where one piece of writing ends and the next one begins.

The full stop

This mark is the most important of all. That's because the sentence is the crucial structural element of all written language. Each one starts with a capital letter and ends with a full stop. This much, at least, we learn at primary school. Later, we learn that some sentences – questions and exclamations – have different marks to end them (see below).

All would be well was it not for the fact that very few pieces of writing contain only a single sentence. The problem which many writers have in using the full stop is that they fail properly to signal where one sentence ends and the next one begins. Either they leave out the full stop and run two sentences together, or they put in a full stop where they don't need one. They need to learn how to distinguish one written sentence from the next.

This becomes particularly important when one sentence has itself been constructed by joining two or more sentences together. When this happens, the original sentences come to be known as 'clauses', the new, enlarged sentence containing two (or more) clauses which, before they were combined together, were themselves single-clause sentences.

The design rules of the language allow for three possibilities in the construction of sentences:

Type A: Sentences with only a single clause
Type B: Sentences with two or more clauses in a coordinated chain
Type C: Sentences with main clause and subordinated clause(s).

If you are not used to studying the way language structure operates, work through the explanations and examples below slowly and carefully, going back and repeating each one if at first it confuses you. (It will come to make sense, but you may need to take it slowly.)

'Type A' sentences

These are easy. We need not dwell for long on Type A sentences. That sentence was a Type A sentence. It had only one clause. So did that one. All the sentences in this paragraph contain only one clause. Each one ends with a full stop.

The simplest way to arrange sentences together, then, is to line them up in a row with a full-stop between each one:

> Here IS the first sentence. This IS sentence number two. Now here IS sentence three. Now we ARE into sentence four. The next sentence WILL BE number six. That WAS the fifth sentence.

If you adopt this system, you are unlikely to make many

punctuation errors. You may, however, drive your reader insane.

The words in bold capital letters are essential to the making of any sentence. They are the 'main verbs' of the sentence. Remember this, because below you will be looking at sentences with more than one verb and we need a means of distinguishing between the main verb and all the others. This will be shown by putting all verbs in capitals but making the main verbs **bold** in addition.

'Type B' sentences

For most purposes, language works in much more complicated ways. Sentences like the ones above need to be combined with others and the most straightforward way of doing so is to join them together with a word like 'and';

> I quite LIKE coffee *and* I really LIKE tea.
>
> He ENJOYS beer *but* he CAN'T STAND cider.
>
> Sam MUST HAVE his cocoa *or* he FEELS depressed.

The three words 'and', 'but', and 'or' (called co-ordinators) link what were originally separate sentences (now clauses) into a chain of co-ordinated parts, all inside the new, larger, sentence, and the process of linking in this way can go on indefinitely;

> We went to Birmingham <u>and</u> we followed that up with a visit to Leeds <u>and</u> then we decided to try Liverpool <u>and</u> after that we took a train down to London <u>and</u> then we went home to Vladivostok.

All one sentence – though once again the result is monotonous. It may even remind you of the kind of writing you used to do many years ago as a young child. If so, it's not surprising; it's the first way in which children learn to join two or more spoken sentences together into one big one, and at first they tend to overdo things. As they come to learn the new technique of putting full stops into their writing, they also make use of this well-established speech strategy, using both kinds of boundary-marker at once. We find writing like this:

> Yesterday we went to see my Aunty. And she lives in a big house by the seaside. And we started off early in the morning. And my aunty is called Aunty Doreen.

It's a way of making doubly certain that the boundary

between each sentence is undeniably seen to be there. The result can be the teacher's injunction: 'Never start a sentence with "and"!' (After all, if you have a full-stop between sentences, why should you need an 'and' as well?)

'Type C' sentences

There are more complicated ways of putting clauses together than this, however. They involve joining them in a 'subordinated' relationship, like this:

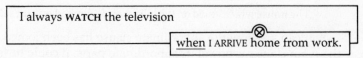

As before, we find two clauses joined together inside a single, multi-clause, sentence. The word 'when' (called a 'subordinator') marks the join and the clauses are now known as the 'main clause' and the 'subordinate clause' respectively. There are now *two* verbs, of course: one in each clause. The one in the main clause is the main verb (bold).

Here are some more examples: the main clauses (always at the highest level) are in bold print; the subordinators are underlined. The subordinate clauses (which can come before, after or as interruptions to the main clause) are printed on a lower, subordinate, level.

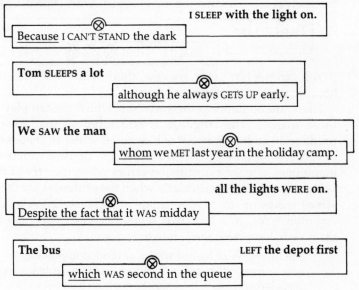

It is quite possible to put a subordinate clause inside another subordinate clause:

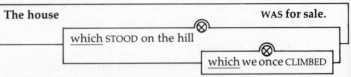

though the second 'which' is likely to be left out of the second subordinate clause:

The house which stood on the hill we once climbed **was for sale**.

You can see how the subordinate clause has been joined to the main clause as one of its subordinate parts. It could be left out, leaving only the main clause as a free-standing sentence, though this process cannot be reversed – try it.

It's also possible to have variations on the two last sentence types: a co-ordinated sentence in which one or more of the clauses itself contains a subordinate clause (Type B with Type C):

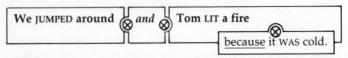

or a sentence in which two or more subordinate clauses are themselves co-ordinated together (Type C with Type B):

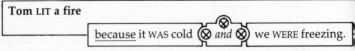

You can see how, in every case, there is only one full stop, because there is only one sentence.

There are no limits to the variations which we can play on these themes. The language is structured so that we can produce an endless number of individual sentence shapes out of very few basic designs. Perhaps because of these variations, many people make punctuation errors when they try to link sentences together, particularly when the sentences are themselves made up from more than one clause. Look at this common error, in which two sentences, each with its own main verb, have been made into one:

The invention of barbed-wire was of vital importance in the development of America, it allowed settlers to fence round much larger tracts of land in a shorter time than before.

Here are the two sentences again, this time with their main verbs in bold capitals:

> The invention of barbed-wire **WAS** of vital importance in the development of America. It **ALLOWED** settlers to fence round much larger tracts of land in a shorter time than before.

The one sentence should have become two and the comma, therefore, should have been a full stop. Alternatively, if the writer had been determined to write just one sentence, he should have joined the two like this, with a subordinator in place of the comma:

> The invention of barbed-wire **WAS** of vital importance in the development of America because it **ALLOWED** settlers to fence round much larger tracts of land in a shorter time than before.

Here's another typical error:

> The Scottish architect and designer Mackintosh is regarded today as one of the major founders of the modernist movement, although he was not recognised during his life-time, he later grew to hold a major reputation especially in his innovatory design for the Glasgow School of Art.

The writer has become confused. The problem has come in the subordinate clause 'although he was not recognised during his life-time'. To which sentence should it belong? The answer is a matter of choice for the writer, but the original punctuation error seems to have occurred because he couldn't make up his mind.

There are two ways this problem could be resolved:

> The Scottish architect and designer Mackintosh **IS REGARDED** today as one of the major founders of the modernist movement, although he **WAS NOT RECOGNISED** during his life-time. He later **GREW TO HOLD** a major reputation, especially in his innovatory design for the Glasgow School of Art.

> The Scottish architect and designer Mackintosh **IS REGARDED** today as one of the major founders of the modernist movement. Although he **WAS NOT RECOGNISED** during his life-time, he later **GREW TO HOLD** a major reputation, especially in his innovatory design for the Glasgow School of Art.

Here's another error, this time caused as the result of too many subordinate clauses:

> At the end of the Second World War, Germany was in ruins. Which paradoxically is one reason why nowadays West Ger-

many is so wealthy because the Allied Powers spent considerable sums of money in helping Germany to rebuild itself.

The problem here is a confusion over the function of the subordinators 'which' and 'because'. Here, the first is allowed to begin a new sentence where it would have been better to keep it within the first, like this:

> At the end of the Second World War, Germany WAS in ruins, which paradoxically IS one reason why nowadays West Germany IS so wealthy because the Allied Powers SPENT considerable sums of money in helping Germany to rebuild itself.

However, there is still some sorting out to do and the sentence would be better being split into two:

> At the end of the Second World War, Germany WAS in ruins. Paradoxically, this IS one reason why nowadays West Germany IS so wealthy, because the Allied Powers SPENT considerable sums of money in helping Germany to rebuild itself.

But you may consider that 'this is one reason why' and 'because' both say the same thing and that therefore either could do the work of both. The sentences would be better still like this:

> At the end of the Second World War, Germany WAS in ruins. Paradoxically, this IS one reason why nowadays West Germany is so wealthy, the Allied Powers having spent considerable sums of money in helping Germany to rebuild itself.

In this case, the subordinate clause in the second sentence has been subordinated to the main clause not by using the subordinator 'because' but by changing the form of the verb itself, 'spent' becoming 'having spent' – another method of subordination.

From now on in your reading, learn to pay special attention to the way sentences have been constructed. It will help you to become accustomed to the full stop and, as it happens, it may also help you with the sentence constructions themselves.

The comma

Where full stops mark the boundaries between sentences, commas mark the boundaries between elements of language *within* sentences.

You can use them to separate off the words in a list:

I **hopped, skipped, ran, jumped and danced** to church.

Notice that the last word in the list of verbs here is not separated with a comma like the others since the word 'and' does the same job (just like 'and' between clauses in a sentence).

You can use commas between phrases in exactly the same way as with single words:

I **tried to hop, attempted a skip, stumbled a run, made a rough apology for a jump and a laughable parody of a dance** to church.

Once again, the last two items in the list ('a rough apology for a jump' and 'a laughable parody of a dance') are separated not by a comma but by the word 'and'.

The separating function of commas can be similar to that of another mark, dealt with later, which is the bracket. In fact, brackets are really 'strong' commas, signalling parenthesis even more forcefully than do those. In the last sentence but one, the phrase 'dealt with later' is separated off from the main body of the sentence by commas. Any unit of language which is interposed into the sentence in this way can be isolated by putting commas round it.

The last time I saw him, **that day soon after Christmas in 1986**, he was slightly drunk and laughing loudly.

If you were to read this sentence aloud, you would almost certainly parenthesise the words between commas by making a slight pause before and after them. Note, however, that the 'pause rule' is not a hard-and-fast one here. It is likely, but not obligatory. Better to *see* the written sentence rather than try to *hear* it when you are making decisions about punctuation.

Sometimes, however, using commas signals an important aspect of the meaning and so a pause in speech would definitely be necessary. Compare these two sentences, reading them aloud:

My sister who lives in Colchester drives a white Volvo.

My sister, who lives in Colchester, drives a white Volvo.

In the first, there are no commas. This suggests that the person writing has more than one sister. Consequently, he is distinguishing her from his other sisters (the ones living in Stockport, Birmingham and Glasgow) by saying where she lives. In the second sentence, however, the phrase is parenthesised in commas. This suggests that he has only one sister and that he is offering the information about where she lives not because it is crucial in identifying the sister but simply to tell his reader more about her. In *saying* these two sentences, we would pause slightly in the second one before and after the phrase 'who lives in Colchester'.

Often, commas are used near the beginning of sentences (like this one) in which an introductory word, phrase or clause is used:

> **Unfortunately,** I am unable to meet you tomorrow.
>
> **As a matter of fact,** we sold the last one yesterday.
>
> **Therefore,** the whole thing will have to be cancelled.
>
> **Until you stop bothering him,** I shan't speak to you.
>
> **When you have finally made your decision,** perhaps you would be kind enough to let me know.

The same thing can happen at the end of a sentence, though now the tendency is weaker:

> I don't enjoy asparagus, **actually**.
>
> There wasn't much point, **to be perfectly frank.**
>
> He couldn't contemplate such a thing, **however.**

Many readers would find the last example clumsy.

In

> It was running out of control, **until he switched it off.**

you can choose, again depending on the fine shade of meaning you wish to express. Contrast that sentence with this one:

> It was running out of control until he switched it off.

You should here detect a greater closeness between the two events described (the running out of control and the switching it off) and therefore less urgency. When they are separated by a comma, there is a greater sense of abruptness. This is an example of how the rules which govern the use of the comma (unlike those for full stops) are not always absolute. You have a choice, and you can exert control over the subtler aspects of your meaning by exercising it.

The colon

Colons announce lists:

The bag was filled with the following items: **apples, a bottle of gin, three books, my wrist-watch, a copy of last week's *Beekeepers' Companion*, two very small pocket calculators and a purple truncheon.**

In this way, they act as boundary-markers between the list itself and the rest of the sentence in which the list occurs.

They also introduce explanations, propositions and ideas:

One can understand the process in the following way: . . .

I should like to propose the following course of action: . . .

Let us consider the suggestions below: . . .

the boundary-marking function still effecting the separation between the explanation and the rest of the sentence in which it occurs.

Sometimes, such an introduction of an idea or proposition is much less obvious, though a colon is still used:

They are rather like human beings: **every one unique.**

where the colon implies the words:

. . . in the following way . . .

You may have noticed that they are also used throughout this chapter to introduce examples, as in the one below:

The colon is used as follows: **to introduce examples, as in the one above.**

The semi-colon

If you aren't confident about using this punctuation mark, don't. Though it has its devotees, there are as many who would say that it is really unnecessary, achieving no more than does the full stop. Though a harsh judgment on this mark, which many find enables them to express subtle relationships of meaning between clauses, it is true that most of what can be achieved with a semi-colon can equally well be achieved with a full stop and therefore the less-than-confident writer would be well advised to leave its use to those who really enjoy that kind of thing. If, however, you are determined to make it part of your repertoire, read on.

A rough-and-ready definition of a semi-colon is that it is a 'weak' full stop. Use it when you want to signal the boundary between two clauses which are of sufficiently close relationship to belong within the same sentence, but which are far enough apart not to be connected with a co-ordinator like 'and' or a subordinator like 'while'.

> She moved slowly towards the door while her husband walked to the window.
>
> She moved slowly towards the door; her husband walked to the window.
>
> She moved slowly towards the door. Her husband walked to the window.

These three examples show the process of separation, from the first, in which the actions of wife and husband are linked explicitly by 'while', to the third, in which the two actions are now quite separate, any link between them being made by inference in the reader's mind. The middle example tries to establish a position mid-way between those two, suggesting both the unity of the two events (existing together within the same sentence as opposed to being each in its own) but at the same time establishing their separateness as well. For such purposes as this, the semi-colon can be a subtle and delicate instrument in your writing.

A further use for the semi-colon is to act as a 'strong' comma. Especially in lists where the items listed are themselves clauses, a semi-colon is often felt to do the job better than a comma, particularly where those clauses themselves contain commas:

> Before setting off, they each packed their personal belongings. Sheila loaded up the tent and all the camping gear; Daniel went off on a brief sortie in search of firewood to be carried on the roof of the Land Rover; Jake made a last round of the traps he had set the night before, finding nothing; Sarah checked all the filming equipment.

Once again, full stops would do just as well here – except that we should then lose the sense that all this activity, this complex event, was happening at the same time within the one, busy sentence.

The bracket

Brackets are (as you might expect) useful for separating stretches of language. Used to put words, phrases, sentences (and even whole paragraphs) into parenthesis, a common punctuation mistake can occur at the point where they close. Remember that, if a sentence opens *inside* brackets, then it must close in them too:

> The best way to get to London is to take the train. (This, of course, assumes you haven't got a car.) Then you can take the tube to Heathrow.

The sentence-mark (full stop, question mark or exclamation mark) which ends the sentence inside the brackets belongs to that sentence and so belongs *inside* the brackets.

However, if a sentence begins *outside* the brackets, with the brackets closing after the last word of the sentence, then the sentence-mark will occur outside the closing bracket:

> When you get to Heathrow, follow the signs for Terminal Three (assuming you are travelling to the USA).

This is because the sentence-mark belongs to the *whole* sentence and not just to the part within brackets.

The same is true in a sentence where the bracketed words come before a comma:

> After you have checked your baggage into the departure desk (the first thing you come to when you enter the terminal), you may have to wait for a while in the lounge.

Take away the bracketed part of the sentence and you can see that the comma would still be needed. In other words, it belongs to the sentence *outside* the brackets, not inside them.

Finally, try to avoid 'nesting' brackets. It may be acceptable in mathematics (where a different kind of language (one which has its own rules, symbols and systems (not forgetting that English is itself a 'system of systems')) is operating) but it can be confusing in normal written English.

The dash

Dashes – and there are many of them in this book – give you the chance to separate the words inside them from the main body of the sentence.

They can be used in *pairs* to fulfil much the same function as a pair of brackets or of commas:

> The ferry was due to depart – whether or not there were any passengers aboard – at 8.30 that evening.

> He arrived with his children – three unruly boys – in an old and battered lorry.
>
> The Vice Chancellor spread out his fingers – the nails perfectly manicured – on the ancient polished boards of the library floor.

However, they tend to be less formal in style than brackets or commas and so are often used in writing which is more relaxed – even conversational – in tone.

Single dashes are also used to mark off the last part of a sentence from the rest:

> She promised to come again on Wednesday – her day off.
>
> Lord Dalgleish stepped back, better to see the flag on top of the church tower, and in doing so brought his heel down squarely in the middle of the Raspberry Surprise – laid lovingly on the cloth by Perigrew a moment earlier.

In the first example, you can see that the dash acts rather like a colon in that it introduces an added explanation. In the second, used in place of a comma, it helps to separate the two incidents – of Perigrew placing the cake on the cloth and its unhappy fate. Contrast this with the subtly different meaning of the sentence without its dash:

> Lord Dalgleish stepped back, better to see the flag on top of the church tower, and in doing so brought his heel down squarely in the middle of the Raspberry Surprise laid lovingly on the cloth by Perigrew a moment earlier.

It would be mistaken, however, to use dashes in place of commas which separate items in a list. These don't look right at all:

> The room was full of old – dusty – neglected – damaged telephones.
>
> It had been a long – hard – exhausting – dangerous evening.

Dashes used like this simply give an impression of breathlessness.

The dash is not an obligatory punctuation mark. Its functions can just as well be performed by other marks, as you can see from the examples. Therefore its use is mainly interesting for the *stylistic* qualities it can add to a written text. In college writing, use it sparingly since some readers may be irritated by its jaunty – even rakish – informality.

Attitude marker

The exclamation mark

This is an unusual punctuation mark. In terms of its structural function, it works in exactly the same way as the full stop, but its main use is that of reinforcing the attitude expressed in the sentence.

These attitudes vary, but are all what might be termed 'excitement' attitudes (though whether 'God, I'm so bored!' breaks this rule is for you to judge). The mark expresses anger, for example:

> I've told you a hundred times never to do that!

or distaste:

> I can't stand semolina pudding!

or sadness:

> I feel so terribly defeated these days!

or delight:

> Suddenly, the colours have come back into my life!

It can also express fascination:

> What an extraordinary invention!
> How remarkable to think that he witnessed it all!

or reinforce the strength behind an order:

> Sit down at once!

or support a warning:

> Look out! Behind you!

You will have noticed that, where attitude is expressed, it is that of the writer which is being supported by the exclamation mark, no one else's. Use of the mark is not so comfortable when those sentences are written of other people's feelings . . .

> She feels so very depressed these days!

unless, of course, these words appear within inverted commas as a direct quotation. In that case, it is the quoted speaker's attitude which is being supported by the mark, not the writer's.

You may be thinking that all these examples are closer to the language of speech than of writing. Use of the exclamation mark is, indeed, less than common in written language and should be used sparingly. In particular, avoid this kind of excess:

> Sensitive town planning seems to have given way these days to no more than a desire for quick profits!!!

or this:

> What kind of politician could have thought up such a dastardly scheme?!?!

The exclamation mark is like a particularly strong and pungent spice: it should be used sparingly for the best effect. Used in the kind of writing you will do in college, it is likely to be very rare indeed. If you find yourself using it, be careful! Are you sure that you aren't getting over-excited?

Labelling marks

A labelling mark is one which gives the word, phrase or sentence to which it is attached a particular characteristic – labelling it as having certain properties which would not always be evident without that label.

The apostrophe

There are two kinds of apostrophe (or, if you prefer, one kind serving two different purposes). The mark about to be described is the 'possessive' apostrophe. Followed by 's' when it is used with nouns, it labels the fact that the noun now expresses possession:

> I could see **Jonathan's** legs.

Certain rules apply to the use of this apostrophe which can sometimes confuse writers. (In fact, there is an increasingly defeatist tendency among some bad writers it leave it out altogether.) Notice that when the possessive apostrophe is used with *plural* nouns, it normally moves to the end of the word:

> Mark heard a thundering of **horses'** hooves.

However, when the noun already expresses the plural, the apostrophe reverts to its normal position before the 's'.

I love **children's** stories.

I get fed up with **people's** bad temper.

Another problem can sometimes occur when the noun already ends in 's', especially when it is a proper noun (a name). Do we write 'Keats's poetry' or 'Keats' poetry'? Probably the first is to be preferred, but to many speakers it sounds awkward. Here is an example, then, of where punctuation is decided on personal preference rather than hard-and-fast rules.

Writers can sometimes confuse the possessive apostrophe with the one used for the different function of deletion (see below), especially in the case of 'it'. If you tend to do this, here's the rule:

It is becomes **it's**.

The thing belonging to it becomes **its thing**.

Here is a list which should make it clear:

It's my book. It's mine.

It's your book. It's yours.

It's his book. It's his.

It's her book. It's hers.

It's its book. It's its. (unlikely!)

It's our book. It's ours.

It's your book. It's yours.

It's their book. It's theirs.

It's whose book? It's the Queen's.

Note that in no case except the Queen's does the possessive apostrophe occur. Remember this one, however:

. . . putting one's life in danger.

The question mark

Since it marks the boundary between one sentence and another, the question mark is a special kind of full stop, but with the added function of labelling the fact that the sentence concerned has been asking a question. (In some languages, the mark is also placed at the *beginning* of the sentence concerned – perhaps a more sensible arrangement.) The fact that a sentence has been asked is usually obvious from the structure of the sentence itself. Notice the word order and other features in the examples below, all of which show the different ways of making questions allowed to us by the grammar of English:

> Who was the man in the red suit? ('wh' question)
> Was the man in the red suit a friend of yours? ('yes/no' question)
> That man was a dentist, wasn't he? ('tag' question)
> Was he wearing green or red? ('either/or' question)

One other question-type, however, is not obvious in writing because grammatically it has just the same structure as a normal statement sentence. In speech, we would signal such a question by our intonation. In writing, this cannot be done and so the question mark becomes essential as a labelling device:

> A: He's fallen in the water.
> B: He's fallen in the water?
> A: Yes – he's fallen in the water.

We sometimes need to make decisions about whether or not to use the question mark, especially when writing in a conversational style.

> You're not cold.

is a statement.

> Surely you're not cold?

is also constructed like a statement, though its intention is to ask a question. Hence the question mark.

Inverted commas

Inverted commas are always used as a pair. They are sometimes called 'quotation marks' or 'speech marks'. When put around any stretch of written language, they label the fact that it is spoken or written by someone other than the writer (except, of course, in the case of a writer quoting him- or herself).

> 1.   'It wasn't very exciting,' I remarked.
> 2.   'Look out!' she screamed.
> 3.   'Where are you now?' wondered Peter.

Notice the rather complicated punctuation which accompanies use of the inverted commas. In [1] the spoken sentence begins with a capital letter, but ends with a comma – not a full-stop – since the complete sentence isn't over until later.

Furthermore, the next letter outside the closed inverted comma is not capital but lower-case, because the whole sentence hasn't yet ended. Always use a comma when a quoted sentence is embedded inside a longer sentence like this, unless the quoted sentence is an exclamation [2] or a question [3] (in which case use one of the alternative sentence-marks).

4. My aunt had written, 'I've gone to the shops.'
5. The vicar murmured, 'Shall I meet you in the vestry?'
6. The sergeant bellowed, 'Atten-SHUN!'

Where the quoted sentence comes at the end of the whole sentence [4], [5] and [6], use a comma before opening the inverted comma and begin the quoted sentence with a capital letter. End it with either a full stop, question mark or exclamation mark just before you close the pair depending on what type of quoted sentence it is. In such cases, there's no need for a second full stop outside the inverted commas as well.

7. 'These,' I said, 'are just what she wanted.'
8. 'Why,' asked Anthony, 'didn't you read the instructions?'
9. 'I don't believe,' breathed Sandra, 'that I've ever truly lived before!'

In [7], [8] and [9] the examples show interrupted quoted sentences – a more complex way of doing things. Since the quoted sentence doesn't end at the interruption, use a comma before the first closure of inverted commas to show that the sentence will be continued later. Open them again as in [4], [5] and [6]. Finally, end with the appropriate sentence-mark in the normal way.

10. She thought, 'I'll see to it later,' and carried on with her letter.
11. They shouted, 'Down with the Dictator!' while they marched towards the Palace.
12. He asked, 'Could you tell me where to find Sue?' and offered the man his map.

In [10], [11] and [12] we have three quoted sentences interrupting the outer sentence, which continues still further after the quoted sentence has finally ended. Notice that exclamations and questions are labelled as such when they finish, but statements, since they are not finishing the whole sentence, end in a comma before the inverted comma, just as they did in [1].

You can, of course, embed statements, questions or exclamations inside sentences which are themselves questions or exclamations:

> Did you say, 'Who are you?' just then?
>
> How strange to say, 'What a mess!' like that!

We should not forget double inverted commas. These can mean exactly the same as the single ones (while using more ink). There are several alternative uses, however. One is for quoting the titles of printed texts, plays, operas, etc:

> I have recently been reading "Lord of the Flies".

though a preferable convention is simply to underline titles.

Sometimes, they are used to distinguish between quoted speech and quoted writing, the latter (unlike the former) being enclosed in double inverted-commas.

Another use is to distinguish between two quoted sentences, one inside the other:

> I said, 'She said, "I wrote it".'

though, for obvious reasons, this isn't often indulged in.

The marks can be used to label the stretch of language they enclose (usually a single word or phrase) as normally being unacceptable in the context – for example, the use of informal, slang terms in a more formal piece of writing;

> The purpose of the game is to score a goal, or "put the ball in the back of the net".

They can show that the enclosed language is used in a way to which you wish to call particular attention because of its style;

> She exhibited a certain "joie de vivre" in her dress, her walk and her manner.

They can also enclose language which is used in a technical sense, drawing the reader's attention to a new term or an unusual use of such a term;

> He accused the chairman of "jerrymandering".

Sometimes, the mark is used to pour scorn on what someone else has said or written;

> Having been to a performance of Beethoven's "Choral Symphony", he said he enjoyed going to "musicals".

Beware of using these marks to apologise for your own choice of words;

Shakespeare makes it clear that Hamlet "fancies" Ophelia.

If you have used a word which you think may need this kind of apology, change the word for one which doesn't.

Single or double? Some people use precisely the opposite system to the one explained above, using double inverted commas for quotations and single ones for the special cases just listed. You will see, if you look in most books printed in British English, that the way illustrated here is preferred. In handwritten English, however, you may decide upon the alternative. Ultimately, the choice is yours – double/single or single/double – as long as you preserve the distinction explained here.

Deletion mark

The apostrophe

There is only one deletion mark: the second of the apostrophes. The deletion apostrophe tells us that part of a word has been left out:

I'm in the garden.

where the letter 'a' has been deleted from the verb 'am', which has then been joined to the pronoun 'I' (a process called 'contraction').

Contraction happens all the time in speech, but some writers feel that the less conversational language used in written English means that contractions are stylistically inferior. However, others will argue that the best writing is that which sounds most natural when it is read aloud and they will be quite happy using the deletion apostrophe freely in their writing. The best policy is one of balance. Feel your way into knowing when it is, and isn't, appropriate. In the case of college assignments, err on the side of not contracting rather than the other way round, but don't make your writing too stilted by leaving it out of your repertoire altogether.

Here are some common uses of the deletion apostrophe. In some cases, you'll notice a change in the shape of the verb which has been contracted.

I'm . . . I am	**you'd** . . . you had (You'd better watch out!)
you're . . . you are	
he's . . . he is *or* he has (He's had a terrible night.)	it **can't** . . . it cannot/it can not
	we'll . . . we will
she's . . . she is *or* she has	I **won't** . . . I will not
it's . . . it is	I **shan't** . . . I shall not
it **isn't** . . . it is not	you **shouldn't** . . . you should not
who's . . . who is	
we're . . . we are	**they've** . . . they have
you **aren't**/**you're** not . . . you are not	he **mustn't** . . . he must not
	it **might've** . . . it might have (unusual in writing)
they're . . . they are	
doesn't . . . does not	we **mightn't've** . . . we might not have (NO!)
don't . . . do not	
wouldn't . . . would not	

In connection with the last two in that list, beware of *might of, would of* and *should of*. Some people still (carelessly) write these as contracted forms of *might have, would have* and *should have*. In written language, the correct form is *would've*, etc, though despite its correctness such a contraction would be inappropriate for all but the most informal written style.

*

This chapter has tried to demonstrate how each of the major punctuation marks is used and also to explain their place in the punctuation system of English writing. If you have studied the chapter, you should not only understand more clearly how to use each mark, but also be able to compare your own use with the examples given. Are there differences? If so, might it be because you are working with a slightly different system, or with a system that is obscured from view, or even – in a hit-and-miss way – with no system at all?

It might encourage you to know that, in preparing this chapter, occasional disagreements occurred between the authors about the use of particular marks. We had to conclude that, while we could be sure in most cases of the correct use of a mark, there were always those interesting exceptions which prove that the rules are not equally strict throughout the punctuation system. This system exists on a gradient of precision; at the one end, rules which all writers must obey if they are to write correctly; at the other, the freedom to use the mark in order to express subtle textures in the meaning and shifts of style.

If punctuation has given you problems in the past, start work on those marks (like the full stop) over which you have no choice. Then practise the ones on which you can exercise more discretion. Experiment with your sentences to see whether your use of a mark changes – however subtly – the meaning you express. Once you begin to feel confident about the effects that punctuation can have upon meaning, you may also find an increased enjoyment in writing. This is because you will be writing not only more correctly, but with a keener sense of style.

Paragraphs

———◆———

A paragraph is a collection of sentences.

That paragraph was one sentence long. It said what was needed and then stopped. This point is made because many people think that a paragraph has an ideal (but mysterious) length. At intervals of about a quarter of a page, they feel it must be time for a new paragraph and so they start the next one. This is not, however, the best system to use. A paragraph, like each of its sentences, is as long as it needs to be to express its meaning. The fact that, in so much of the writing you will read in books, paragraphs tend to happen between three and five times on every page is a matter mainly of *meaning* and partly of *style*. Above all, the paragraph is a unit of the *structure* of a piece of writing: a group of written sentences which has been separated off from other such groups by indentation or by leaving an empty line after it ends.

Style

Paragraphs can have an impact upon the style of the writing. This is not a major part of their function, but is nonetheless one worth bearing in mind. Paragraphs split up a page of writing into smaller chunks. Depending on the size of the chunks, the writer is able to establish a *rhythm* on the page, and this can sometimes be an important aspect of the style he or she is attempting to achieve. A slow, deliberate, reflective, detailed style may in part be accomplished by using long paragraphs, ones which take their time. A breathless, urgent, excited style might be better achieved, however, with short, sharp paragraphs, many to the page. The first might be particularly appropriate to writing in which a carefully-detailed argument is being established; the second, to the climax of an action-packed thriller or an advertisement.

There are dangers, however, in such a stylistic device. The page littered with a sequence of brief paragraphs can seem bitty and lacking in substance. By contrast, the one which is loaded down with a single block of print can sometimes leave the reader feeling stranded half way through, eyes straying to the foot of the page in the hope of seeing a way out from this dense jungle of words. It is as much the space between paragraphs as the paragraphs themselves which can matter: the mind needs somewhere to rest momentarily before embarking on the next part of the writing and the end of a paragraph is one such resting-place – providing, of course, that the resting-place relates to the meaning.

Structuring the meaning

The meaning of a piece of writing can be broken down into (or built up from) its individual elements – each self-contained, but at the same time related to all the others within the complete structure. Paragraphs have their place within this set of structural language elements:

book
part
chapter
section
sub-section
PARAGRAPH
sentence
clause
phrase
word

Of course, not all pieces of writing will use every one of these elements. Few people write complete books while at college, and what occurs higher in this hierarchy than the words, phrases, clauses and sentences in the structure of your college writing will depend on the nature of your summary, essay, report, etc. Nonetheless, the typical college essay is, in many ways, like the chapter of a book: not the whole story, but a considered, detailed, and relatively self-contained part of it. So sub-sections and sections, would be likely. The 'long essay' or 'dissertation' will have more than one chapter and may even contain several 'parts', as well as the elements lower down in level.

The structure of a paragraph

Paragraphs also have a structure and writing becomes better-shaped when writers think about the structure of their paragraphs.

Just as a complete piece of writing is likely to have a beginning, a middle and an end, so will a paragraph, and in this it is like a complete text in miniature. A text may, for example, have an 'introduction', a 'development' and a 'conclusion'; so may a paragraph. A complete text may start off by making a major point (perhaps its first chapter), to be followed by chapters which develop it; so may a paragraph. Alternatively, a complete text may not come to its main point until the end; as may a paragraph. Many texts will be concerned with the qualifications and alternatives to the heart of their arguments; as may a paragraph. And just as a complete text will end in some conclusion, a paragraph can often be brought to an end with some concluding re-statement of the main point made earlier on.

If there is a difference (apart from length and complexity) between the structure of a complete text and that of an individual paragraph, it will be in the fact that where, in a complete text, there may be a great many 'main points', in a paragraph there is generally only one. This is crucial to understanding what paragraphs are and how they work. Each paragraph has one main point. When all that there is to say about this point has been said, the paragraph ends and a new one begins. So when you construct your own paragraphs, consider whether you have made its main point clearly enough, or whether there are two or more main points struggling with each other within the same paragraph for space to breathe.

To illustrate the idea, look again at that last paragraph, this time broken down into its sentences to show its structure.

1   If there is a difference (apart from length and complexity) between the structure of a complete text and that of an individual paragraph, it will be in the fact that where, in a complete text, there may be a great many 'main points', in a paragraph there is generally only one.

2   This is crucial to understanding what paragraphs are and how they work.

3   **Each paragraph has one main point**.

4   When all that there is to say about this point has been said, the paragraph ends and a new one begins.

5   So when you construct your own paragraphs, consider whether you have made its main point clearly enough, or whether there are two or more main points struggling with each other within the same paragraph for space to breathe.

The third sentence of the paragraph contains its main point and the structure of this particular paragraph places the main point centrally, right at its heart. Two sentences lead up to it, and two more lead away from it to the conclusion, in a structure like an hour-glass. In the first sentence, the point of the previous paragraph (that paragraphs are comparable in structure to complete texts) is re-stated in order to make a contrast (the phrase 'If there is a difference . . .' alerting you to expect one). The contrast clears the way for sentence 3 by establishing this difference between a complete text and an individual paragraph. Sentence 2 tries to underline the point; it looks back to sentence 1 and at the same time forward to the main point in sentence 3. Sentence 4 further reinforces the point in sentence 3. Sentence 5 tries to make a generalised statement arising out of the first four sentences (the word 'So' alerting the reader to a conclusive statement). It also makes the main point more personal by showing you, the reader, how it can be applied in your own writing, offering an indication of how a failure to observe the point could cause confusion. The structure of that particular paragraph could be shown like this:

Link with previous paragraph (sentence 1)
Bridge-sentence from 1 to 3 (sentence 2)
Main point (sentence 3)
Reinforcement (sentence 4)
Conclusion (sentence 5)

Here's another example:

1 That paragraph was one sentence long.

2 It said what was needed and then stopped.

3 This point is made because many people think that a paragraph has an ideal (but mysterious) length.

4 At intervals of about a quarter of a page, they feel it must be time for a new paragraph and so they start the next one.

5 This is not, however, the best system to use.

6 A paragraph, like each of its sentences, is as long as it needs to be to express its meaning.

7 The fact that, in so much of the writing you will read in books, paragraphs tend to happen between three and five times on every page is a matter mainly of meaning and partly of style.

8 **Above all, the paragraph is a unit of the structure of a piece of writing: a group of written sentences which has been separated off from other such groups by indentation or by leaving an empty line after it ends.**

This paragraph builds up to its main point in the final sentence. The first two sentences are short and simple and refer back to the paragraph before (the use of 'That' is a clear pointer). It then comments on *itself* ('This point is made because . . . ') in order to introduce the rest of the paragraph, the first stage in the run-up to the main point. Sentence 4 illustrates sentence 3. Sentence 5 comments on 4. Sentence 6 tries to reinforce the message in sentences 1 and 2. Sentence 7 starts the resulting explanation. The final sentence, 8, comes to the main point. By the time it arrives you as the reader should be in a better position to be able to accept what it says, having already had the alternatives outlined and dismissed.

So the essential structure of that paragraph could be shown like this:

Link with previous paragraph (sentences 1 and 2)
Introduction to main point begins (sentence 3)
Illustration (sentence 4)
Comment (sentence 5)
Reinforcement (sentence 6)
Explanation (sentence 7)
Main point (sentence 8)

Here's an example of a 'springboard' paragraph – one in which the writer sets up a proposition and prepares for the arguments which it suggests. The proposition itself – part of an essay for a politics course – concerns the problems which democratic governments face in dealing with terrorist groups and anti-democratic foreign governments.

> The taking of hostages by foreign powers has thrown into sharp focus a very difficult problem for the western democracies: **whether they should negotiate with powers with which they disapprove** in order to save their own nationals. It is easier to adopt a 'no deals with terrorists' position that it is to adopt a 'no deals with anti-democratic governments' one, but there may often seem to be little difference between them. The situation can place democratic governments in a most uncomfortable position, morally as well as politically.

The writer knows that he wants to examine some opposing arguments:

Should democracies do deals with terrorists and/or anti-democratic governments?

YES	NO
because we might have no real alternative	because it compromises the democratic principle
because dealing with them may persuade them to think and act in ways which we find more acceptable	because, by refusing to do deals, we can force them to change the way they think and act
because we can't just assume that we know best about how to behave and that our way is always right	because it would encourage other blackmail threats against us
because if we refuse to deal with one, we can't really deal with any (which would be foolish)	because doing so would give them a propaganda victory

Having established the proposition (in the paragraph's main point: whether they should negotiate with powers with which they disapprove) the writer was able to spread out these opposed views, sketched in the above notes, into subsequent paragraphs.

Here are the paragraph's sentences (the first one split in half):

1.a   The taking of hostages by foreign powers has thrown into sharp focus a very difficult problem for western democracies:

1.b   whether they should negotiate with powers with which they disapprove in order to save their own nationals.

2.   It is easier to adopt a 'no deals with hostages' position than it is to adopt a 'no deals with anti-democratic governments' one, but there may often seem to be little difference between them.

3.   The situation can place democratic governments in a most uncomfortable position, morally as well as politically.

The paragraph acts not only as the springboard for a longer argument, to be developed in later paragraphs, but also structures *itself* on the same springboard principle, the opening part (sentence 1.a) launching the main point (1.b) and also an idea which is ended in the last sentence:

> The taking of hostages by foreign powers has thrown into sharp focus a very difficult problem for western democracies . . . [placing] democratic governments in a most uncomfortable position, morally as well as politically.

The other sentence ('It is easier . . . difference between them') simply amplifies the idea in the main point. So the structure of this paragraph works like this:

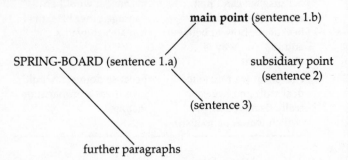

Here's another kind of paragraph – with a structure rather like a 'funnel':

> Science in the twentieth century has been dominated by two theories: <u>relativity</u> and <u>quantum theory</u>. The first deals with the vast: the nature of time and the universe. The second deals with the behaviour of the tiny: atomic particles, for example. Both have completely re-organised our conception of the way things are. However, the two branches of theory are in some ways incompatible and so the problem for scientists is to find a way of reconciling them. To make complete sense of the universe, such a reconciliation must be possible. What we need is a <u>grand unifying theory</u> which would bring the two together. Such a theory would, it is believed, explain – quite literally – everything.

Two ideas 'funnel' their way into one. Each of the *three* notions that are needed to create the paragraph (<u>relativity</u>, <u>quantum theory</u> and the <u>grand unifying theory</u>) must each have its own space, becoming a component part of the 'main point', which in this example is expressed not in any particular sentence but in the paragraph as a whole. In fact, the last sentence, which brings the idea in the paragraph to a conclusion, is in effect a summary of the main point which has been implied throughout: that we can understand everything if we have the right theory. The structure works like this:

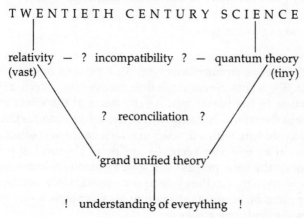

The examples above show how the paragraphs illustrated display different structures. However, there is no 'pattern book' in which you will find an exhaustive list of paragraph structures. Good writers do not shape their paragraphs according to templates which they find in books, polish up, and adapt for their own purposes. They do, however, write with an awareness of the importance of structure, using paragraphs to shape and control their ideas rather than let them straggle down the page without direction. More important than *which* structure a paragraph may have is the fact that it has a structure at all.

Much of the writing done by students suffers because they do not pay enough attention to the ways in which paragraphs are shaped, failing to help their readers find a way to the main point they are trying to express. So by considering *structure* as an important principle in your writing, you will find that you write more clearly and persuasively and, in consequence, that your thinking will be clarified too.

Building it up

Those examples allowed us to take paragraphs to pieces and discover their structure. In the example below, we can see the process in reverse as the writer begins with an idea and builds it into a complete paragraph. She is writing about a complicated process of economics: the effect of the value of the pound on the price of exports. Here are her first-stage notes:

> – £ up – exports down – economic problems – exports up – recovery – £ down –

She needs to describe how, when one thing happens, another set of circumstances result: a process of cause-and-effect. She wants the nature of the process to be reflected in the structure of the paragraph. As she looks at the effect of the value of the pound on the British economy, she can see that she is really dealing with a process in which cause-and-effect goes round in a circle. Her second-stage notes (Figure 1 opposite) elaborate the basic process and start to introduce more detail.

How, though, can the cycle be completed? How can the now low pound be brought up again to an acceptable level? In her notes she finds one answer:

> Q: How to keep £ attractive but not too attractive?
> A: (one way) manipulate INTEREST RATES (Chancellor, Treasury, Bank of England)

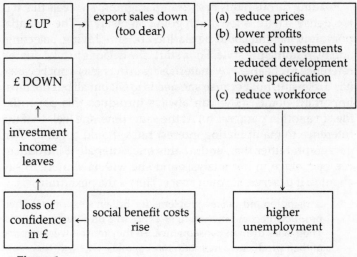

Figure 1

Having sketched out the main idea (its major features and its structure), she now writes her first draft paragraph:

A rising pound makes problems for Britain's exporters. Their products become increasingly expensive on foreign markets. Their sales drop in consequence. So they must lower the price of their products to maintain foreign sales. One way to do so is to use cheaper materials. (Of course, if manufacturers buy their raw materials from overseas, a high pound effectively lowers their costs. In some cases, the lower cost of raw material offsets the higher price of exported goods.) Another is to modify product-design, downgrading its specification. A third is to lay-off part of the labour force. In this way, a strong pound can lead to higher unemployment. However, once unemployment starts to rise, the cost of paying for people who are out of work also rises. All these things can cause investors to be suspicious of the British economy so that they sell their sterling and so its value starts to fall again. This process can lead to a 'run on the pound' and, if its value drops too far, people invest their money elsewhere. As a result, manufacturers cannot find enough money to develop their products, which become out-dated and uncompetitive. Hence, one of the most difficult tasks faced by any Chancellor of the Exchequer is to find the right balance, the best level for the pound which will keep investors happy while at the same time keeping the price of British products abroad competitive. One way to do this is to manipulate the interest rates.

115

Reading through this first-draft paragraph, she feels that it is too dense. There is too much going on inside it. The essential point it is making could be clarified by simplifying, selecting, and by refining the style. For a start, she decides to take out the reference to cheaper raw materials from overseas – not because it is irrelevant, but because she needs to sift out all but the most important points. (She can always introduce this particular idea in another paragraph.) At the same time, she feels that the reference to manipulating interest rates should begin its own paragraph rather than ending this one. After all, it introduces the next stage in her analysis and she will have more to say about it: it deserves its own space. Here's the next draft.

> A rising pound makes problems for Britain's exporters. Their products become increasingly expensive on foreign markets. Their sales drop in consequence. So they must lower the price of their products to maintain foreign sales. One way to do so is to use cheaper materials. Another is to modify product-design, downgrading its specification. A third is to lay-off part of the labour force. In this way, a strong pound can lead to higher unemployment. However, once unemployment starts to rise, the cost of paying for people who are out of work also rises. These things can cause investors to be suspicious of the British economy so that they sell their sterling and so its value starts to fall again. This process can lead to a 'run on the pound' and, if its value drops too far, people invest their money elsewhere. As a result, manufacturers cannot find enough money to develop their products, which become out-dated and uncompetitive.

This still needs work. In particular, the cyclic nature of the process has not been made clear enough. She decides to end the paragraph by bringing it back to the beginning, reflecting in the paragraph structure the shape of the process itself.

> . . . which become out-dated and uncompetitive. To save the situation, the pound must be 'rescued'. Its value then starts to rise once more but, if it rises foo far, the process begins all over again.

Her main point is contained within the first and last sentences, with a linkage in between:

> A rising pound makes problems for Britain's exporters . . . its value starts to fall . . . its value then starts to rise once more, but . . . a rising pound makes problems for Britain's exporters

and so on. The sentences between these points provide the

illustration and explanation for the main point. The shape of the paragraph is like a sandwich, the filling surrounded by the first and last sentences, which hold the whole idea together.

Satisfied with the overall structure, she now feels that more work is needed on the style. Here's the finished paragraph after all the editing has been done (the main idea highlighted in bold type). You can also see how she has moved the next main point (manipulating interest rates) to the start of the next paragraph.

> **As the value of the pound rises relative to other currencies, so the problems mount up for Britain's exporters.** Their products become ever more expensive on foreign markets, their sales drop in consequence, and they are forced to take action to lower the price of their products if they are to continue to export. One way to do so is to use cheaper materials. Another is to modify product-design, downgrading the specification. A third is to lay off part of the labour force, in this way fuelling higher unemployment and causing social benefit costs to rise. These adverse effects cause investors to look with suspicion at the British economy and, as confidence wanes, they start to sell their stock of sterling. As a result, **its value starts to fall** again. However, if this fall becomes a 'run on the pound', and its value drops too far, investment income starts to leave the country for other markets. Manufacturers cannot find sufficient money to invest in developing their products, which become out-dated and uncompetitive. To save the situation, the pound must be 'rescued'; **its value then starts to rise once more** but, if it rises too far, the process begins all over again.
>
> Hence, one of the most difficult tasks faced by any Chancellor of the Exchequer is to find the right balance, the best level for the pound which will keep investors happy while at the same time keeping the price of British products abroad competitive. One way he can do this is to manipulate the interest rates. . . .

Not all her paragraphs go through so many stages. The degree to which she needed to edit this one in order that it should say what she wanted resulted from the complexity of the idea she was trying to express. You will probably find the same to be true in your own writing: some paragraphs flow naturally while others, perhaps containing the core of your thinking, need much more detailed working before they start to look right.

*

117

Now have a look at some of your own paragraphs and see whether you can describe their structures like the examples in this chapter. Look for the different ways in which your paragraphs can be structured (for each is different) and try to discover whether you display a preference for any particular shape. (For instance, do you find you almost always put the main point first?) If you do find such a preference, ask whether this might lead to your paragraphs becoming rather monotonous for the reader and whether you might improve your writing by trying out some variations. Above all, ask whether the structures of your paragraphs adequately reflect the meanings you want to express.

Most importantly, try to find out whether your paragraphs have any clear structure at all. Much writing in college can fail to make itself as clear and effective is it might because the paragraphs contain either no discernible main point, or contain several – with unclear relationships between them.

Connections

This chapter has stressed the importance to good writing of the *internal* shape of paragraphs. However, you will need also to think about the way your paragraphs connect together if your written text is to flow easily and clearly from beginning to end. A paragraph is rarely such a self-contained element of writing that it needs no connections at all with the paragraphs on each side.

Often, the reader can work out the link between paragraphs because of the meaning; at other times, however, it helps if there are words or phrases which make the connections explicit. (The word 'Hence' which joins the two example paragraphs above illustrates the point.) So good writing takes care to make such connections clear when they need to be and 'invisible' when they don't. In the next chapter, you can see how to help your reader find a way around your writing by using 'signposts' which connect the parts together and so help to point the way.

Signposts

◆

Interrogating the text

In travelling through a piece of writing, readers need a guide. After all, reading consists of more than simply putting letters together to make words, phrases and sentences. It is an *active* process which goes far beyond such mechanical decoding. The reader's subconscious mind, as well as the conscious one, is involved in a constant process of questioning. Somewhere in your mind as you read this, you will be asking questions like: 'What's coming into my head here?', 'What does it mean?', 'Does it make sense?', 'What's likely to come next?', 'How does this part relate to that part?' and it is only by asking such questions that you can successfully reconstruct in your mind what I have in mine as I try to express these ideas to you.

Reading has been described as 'interrogating the text' but, if this interrogation is too laborious, the reader becomes confused, irritated, impatient and eventually dismissive. Good writers help their readers by entering into their minds and anticipating the kinds of questions they are likely to ask. What's more, they help them find the answers. This is done in part by offering them 'signposts' to show them the way.

Showing the way

You may be one of those writers who are always being told that your work is 'disorganised' or that it 'lacks clarity and struc-

119

ture'. This could be because your writing is without signposts, and therefore forces your readers to cast around for clues as to where you are taking them. Obviously, careful planning will help. If you used some of the techniques described in 'Starting, planning and finishing', your writing will already begin to take on much greater clarity of structure and direction than if you write it out from the beginning without such planning. There are further features, too, which can help: words and phrases which make evident the lines of connection and direction in a piece of writing. It is surprising how often college writing neglects to use these features, and striking how far they can clarify and so improve the finished results.

Pointing

Some signposts are very common in the language already, in both speech and writing. We take them for granted. They consist of words or phrases which *point*, either backwards or forwards, to other parts of the language-environment. For example, the two sentences below are linked by the pointing-words in **bold type**:

The man in the black coat stood in the middle of the park.

He was waiting **there** for a woman in an orange dress.

'He' and 'there' in the second sentence refer respectively to 'the man in the black coat' and 'the middle of the park' in the first. This capacity of language to refer within itself is called 'reference'. You can see how reference words are obviously of great importance in showing how sentences relate together in meaning. Without them, the sentences in a piece of connected language (a 'text') would fail properly to connect. The sense would start to fall apart and the reader would soon lose the way.

The kinds of writing you will need to do for your college course will, of course, vary according to the different needs of your subject and of the lecturer who has set your assignment. Nonetheless, it is probable that two kinds of signposting in particular will be required whatever you write: those which show **sequence** and those which indicate connections of **logic**. It is surprising how often these are absent from such writing – and how much more difficult, therefore, the writing is to read.

120

Sequence

Sequence is important because you will want to lead your reader in clear stages through your text. The simple addition to your writing of words like 'firstly', 'secondly', 'next', 'lastly', 'in conclusion' make clear to the reader where he or she is.

Sequence may not be quite as straightforward as this suggests, however. After all, you may find that your argument just won't be properly expressed if you simply move through from beginning to end like this. There may be subsidiary points to be made along the way, or you may need to take the reader back in a loop to an earlier point before moving on to the next main idea. If so, use the language at your disposal in order to signpost the fact.

Before considering X, it will be important to look briefly at Y.

signals your intention to move to the next point – but with a detour first.

Having dealt with A, we can now move on to B.

reminds the reader where he or she has just come from and prepares the way for the next stage of the journey.

While remembering (1), we should also bear in mind (2) and (3).

allows the reader to know that you are making two more parallel points to accompany the one you have just made.

Furthermore, we should note that . . .

expresses the fact that an additional point is about to be added to the one just made.

These examples are simple indicators of the ways in which you can clarify the direction and sequence you are taking in your writing. Many a lecturer, piles of scripts still to be marked and midnight approaching, will welcome such guidance.

Logical relationships

Not only sequence: you need also to pay attention to the way your writing builds up a logical argument. How does the meaning of one point relate to another? Does it support it? Contradict it? Qualify it? Lead on from it? It will sometimes be difficult for your reader to know unless you signpost the relationship.

Consequently, it can be seen that . . .

As a result, we can conclude that . . .

Thus, it can be understood that . . .

show how one thing arrives as a result of another. (Be careful, though, to *mean* it: student writing often draws conclusions without any evidence to back them up.)

By contrast, we read that . . .

expresses a changes of direction, a contrasting position.

However, so-and-so says that . . .

suggests an alternative to a proposition, one which is about to be contrasted to it, or to refute it in some way.

Therefore, it should be obvious that . . .

Hence, we can assume that . . .

begins to conclude, perhaps from evidence, that a proposition is true or false.

Nonetheless, we should not forget that . . .

reminds us that there is something else to be taken into account.

Despite the fact that . . .

Although we have seen how . . .

concede that, though some things may hold true, other things need also to be accounted for.

These are all useful illustrations of the ways in which we can signpost such logical relationships, helping the reader to make sense of what may be a complex web of propositions, counter-propositions and subtle relationships of meaning. Yet it is often the unfortunate reader who has to do all the hard work, supplying the signposts by painstakingly trying to guess what was in the writer's mind as the assignment was put together, piece by disconnected piece.

Indentation and numbering

Report writing is rather different. Here, the relationships between the parts and the sequence between them are made explicit by a system of numbering. For example:

1.   FIRST PARAGRAPH (sub-heading)
1.i   . . . First point
1.ii   . . . Second point
1.ii(a)   . . . subsidiary point one
1.ii(b)   . . . subsidiary point two
2.   SECOND PARAGRAPH (sub-heading)
2.i   . . . First point
2.i(a)   . . . subsidiary point one
2.i(b.i)   . . . subsidiary point two [one]
2.i(b.ii)   . . . subsidiary point two [two]
2.ii   . . . second point

and so on. This can get a little wearing, especially when things become complex and one has to refer to 'paragraph 3.i point (a.i.b.ii)' but you can see how, in such writing, the chances of getting completely lost are extremely low. Each numbered point of text is like a map-reference, allowing the reader to move instantly to a part of the writing and to see how it relates to other parts surrounding it. Don't use this method of signposting, however, if you are attempting a fluid, readable style. It is most often used in official reports – writing in which, if nothing else, one has to admire the writer's orderliness of presentation.

Sub-headings

There are other ways to help your reader through your text. In the same way that a book (this one for instance) is divided into ever smaller pieces – parts, chapters, sub-sections, paragraphs – so too your own writing can sometimes benefit from such segmentation. For example, if your essay is structured into parts like these:

Introduction
Main proposition
Counter-propositions
Synthesis of arguments
Conclusion
(References and Bibliography)

then you may find it helps your reader to give each of these sections a separate heading to signpost the fact – though not necessarily with headings as abstract as these.

Furthermore, there may be a case for putting sub-headings within these sections. Look again at pages 5 to 8 of this book. Does the labelling of paragraphs help you, the reader, to reconstruct the whole meaning of that chapter? Even if you think not, your own assignment may well benefit from such labelling – as perhaps this chapter does. Make the experiment. And look through other books to see how their writers signpost these texts for the reader.

Text styles

Even if you choose not to use headings and sub-headings, there are still other ways in which you can assist your reader. Don't forget the uses to which <u>underlining</u> can be put. You may not be fortunate enough to own a word-processor, but if you do, you may also be able to make use of **bold** and *italic* type to highlight and clarify still further parts of your text. (For the handwritten essay, you may find it useful to use different colours in your writing, for example, for quotations. Be careful, though: some lecturers may not take too kindly to being handed a rainbow-coloured script, despite their undoubted desire for constant excitement.)

Graphics

Depending on the kind of writing you are required to do, you should also consider whether the facts and ideas you want to express are best said in words, or whether graphics may do the job more effectively. The graph or diagram, providing it is well-supported by text, can be a much more efficient way of communicating certain ideas than words alone could be. If you do use graphics, don't make the mistake of putting them in a different part of the assignment to the text which refers to them. It is most annoying to have to shuffle between different pages of the writing at the same time. Though you may sometimes puzzle your readers, you should endeavour at all times not to anger them. Essays which are returned bearing toothmarks should give you cause for a thoughtful re-assessment of your approach.

*

Helping your reader by signposting your writing in ways like these has one further great advantage. It will help *you*, as well as your reader. By considering the ways in which you can clearly indicate the process of your thinking from one end of a piece of writing to the other, you are having to clarify your own thinking in the process. You will find, in doing so, that the two essential ingredients of most successful writing in college begin to come together for you:

- clear organisation of your subject matter;
- clear language in which to express it.

Given that you also understand what you are writing about, no lecturer will ask for much more.

Presenting and receiving

$\blacklozenge$

Lecturers can have many things on their minds when they read their students' assignments. Although some may not admit it, the desk piled high with marking is not a place to which many lecturers hurry in gleeful anticipation.

It's not that they have no interest in what students write for them: they do – if only because it will be in this writing that they can see evidence of the success or otherwise of their own teaching. It is certainly not the case that they are professionally careless about their marking; good lecturers take this part of their job very seriously and work hard at it. It is, nonetheless, a task – a batch of assignments can often take a weekend to mark well. Occasionally, this task is made especially worthwhile by the unexpected appearance of a genuinely brilliant piece of work. A little more often, it is made depressing by the appearance of an exceptionally awful one. Normally, however, it is – as you would expect – about average. And most repetitive, average tasks can lose a little lustre after a while.

Keep in mind a psychological point, then: though writing the assignment will have been quite unique in your experience – at its best, the breaking of new ground and a genuine occasion for learning – for the lecturer, it will probably be only one among many. The others on the desk are likely to deal with the same topic as yours. Furthermore, they may be this year's example of an annual crop of writing on a theme which has enriched a lecturer's working life for many years.

You should therefore try to make your lecturer's job as interesting as possible, and if you are rightly modest about your ability to come up with startling new ideas, penetratingly novel insights or a challengingly fresh analysis, at least try to make things easier by presenting your work in the best possible way.

Everything that you have so far read in this book is aimed at that objective. The most effective assistance you can give any reader, especially one who is charged with the responsibility of reading a text carefully, writing comments upon it, correcting its errors and assigning it a grade, is to write what you know after sensible and thorough preparation and planning, with clarity and organisation, and all the while observing the normal conventions of written English.

And there are other things, too, which will make things a little easier and more rewarding for your reader. Style is something which people find it hard to define, but which nonetheless they grumble about when they feel it to be 'clumsy' or 'inappropriate'. Since writing and thinking are so closely related, it could well be that the style of what you write and the clarity and precision of your thinking are not too far apart. Making your style better not only satisfies this particular requirement of your reader but also helps to ensure that your thinking, too, is shapely and elegant.

A most important feature of any college writing is the evidence it offers of your reading. Many assignments have been marked down by lecturers because their writers have shown little evidence of having read the books and articles appropriate to their writing task. (Some show no evidence of having read anything at all.) Alternatively, a written assignment can suffer at the hands of the marker because, although appropriate reading has supported the writing, it has not been presented in an acceptable way. To help you make certain you are not caught out like this, read the chapter 'Quotations, references and bibliographies' – and note especially what is written there about plagiarism, the sin of academic theft. (This, if you do not observe the rules, could cost you your final qualification.)

Presentation can also be a matter of technology. If you are thinking of writing your assignments on a word-processor, read the chapter in this section: there are disadvantages as well as obvious benefits in relying too heavily on these wonderful machines.

And then there's the matter of getting your assignment back

from the lecturer. This is, for many students, a nerve-racking experience. For others, it's of no consequence at all. However, a more constructive way to view it is to see it as the second half of an important transaction between you and your teacher. 'Getting it back' suggests why.

Style

All language has a style

All language, spoken and written, has a style. It can't be avoided. The language style in this example should be instantly recognisable:

> 4 bdm dtchd des res in prime situation close shops and schools. 2 recep. Lge fitted ktchn. Utility rm. Dnstrs shwr. 4-pc bathrm suite (peach). Full gas CH. Dbl glzng throughout. Det. grge. Well-laid gdns front and rear. Must be seen. Offers in region £172,000.

The leaving-out of letters in words, the omission of words (like 'to' and 'the' in 'close shops') together with certain words which are used only in connection with houses, all help to identify this short piece of language as a house-for-sale advertisement in the small-ads column of a local paper. It has the 'des-res' style, and although it would seem very strange to someone who had never seen one before, any house-hunter, having read dozens more just like it, would find it instantly recognisable.

Style, then, is a set of features which characterises *any* piece of language. It isn't possible to find 'style-less' language. Even the most apparently neutral, anonymous language has a style (one we would have to describe as 'neutral and anonymous').

What is 'style' made of?

The difficulty comes in trying to *describe* this style, to show how it differs from any other style and so claims an identity of its own. Many people would say that style in writing (as in most other things) cannot be defined. They talk about it in terms of a 'feeling', an 'essence', a 'quality which you know when you come across it', as if it had been added afterwards to a piece of language like the flavouring in canned soup. But this may mean no more than that they don't know how to define it.

Yet style *can* be defined, though to be precise in your definition may be a highly-skilled activity. (There is even a branch of language study called 'stylistics' which tries to do nothing else.) However, you don't have to go to these lengths to understand the stylistic requirements which you will need to meet in your own written language at college. Finding a sensible, usable, style for your own purposes can be much more straightforward.

Successful style results from two things: the words and how they have been put together, and the social attitudes expressed in the language used.

The words and how they have been put together

Obviously, the substance out of which written style is made is the written language itself: the words and how they have been put together. A particular choice of words, and a particular way of combining them together into sentences, is what will give that piece of language its particular style. (You might also want to add the visual appearance of the language to your assessment of its style: heavy Gothic print, for example, will add something quite different to the style of a piece of writing than would elegant, airy italic script.)

The social attitudes expressed in the language used

Communicating a message in language is a *social* action, an interchange between at least two people. Furthermore, it implies a set of attitudes within the communicated message, attitudes about the *content* of what is being communicated and about the *social relationship* between the sender and its recipients. For the action of communicating to succeed, the method in which it is done, its style, must be *appropriate*.

Here's an example. Two people are together in a room on a cold day. One has just come in, leaving the door open. After a

133

moment, the other one says, 'It's rather chilly in here, isn't it? Would you mind if I closed the door?'

The *intention* behind the message is clear: 'Let's make the room warmer by closing the door'. But there's a social dimension to the action as well: a relationship to be considered between the two people involved. You will probably have gathered from the words which are said that the person saying them is anxious not to offend the one who has left the door open. The words are chosen with care: 'rather chilly' is a gentler description of the temperature than 'very chilly' or 'very cold' or 'freezing' would have been. That sentence is put as a question, giving the other person the chance to disagree ('As a matter of fact, I'm quite warm.'). The second sentence, also a question, gives the second person an opportunity to make his or her own views known by saying, 'Well – yes, I *do* mind, since you ask.' The speaker also offers to close the door him- or herself. Every effort is being made to be polite (and a possible response would be: 'I'm so sorry! Let *me* do it.') Perhaps the two people don't know each other. The language style is matched to a meeting between strangers.

Contrast it with the style of this language in the same situation:

'It's *freezing*! Shut the door for God's sake!'

Now the words are different. They have become more extreme ('freezing' for 'rather chilly' and 'shut' for the gentler 'close'). The questions have become, in the first sentence, a statement of fact (no argument allowed here), and in the second an order (no longer a request to be allowed to perform a service). The tag at the end ('for God's sake!') makes it quite clear that the speaker is in no mood for argument. If the two people were strangers, as before, then the second may well take offence at the abruptness of language in the first. However, if they were good friends, it is unlikely any offence would be taken at all. (The whole thing could be said with broad grins on both sides.)

The examples show us a single event (closing a door in a cold room) in two social situations: one between people who are trying to be polite, the other where politeness is less important.

The language used in each case has been constructed to match the social requirements of the situations concerned. The attitudes are different, so the words and the way they have been put together also differ: same message, different styles.

Writing and talking

Although there are important similarities between writing and talking, there are also many crucial differences between the two ways of making language. Written language is not the same as spoken language and it is wise not to mix up the two if your style is to be successful. People who write as they talk are often poor writers and those who speak as they write are sometimes thought to be pompous and pedantic talkers. The reasons for the differences are many: they arise from the fact that writing and speaking use different language codes; and from the fact that writing and speaking have different functions to play in human society. No matter what is said or written, then, *the very forms of language themselves have different styles*. Problems can occur in students' writing because they have not made a clear enough distinction between them.

Different codes

Writing exists in the medium of vision, speech in the medium of sound.

Writing is normally slower to do than speaking.

Writing has spelling and punctuation; speech doesn't.

There is no stress, intonation, pausing, tone of voice, gesture, body-movement or facial expression in writing; in speech there is.

Speech has many 'mending devices', used when people make mistakes (as they constantly do). These devices mean that, most of the time, people are either unaware of mistakes, or else they don't find they obscure the clarity of the spoken message. In writing, however, the only mending devices available are tippex or a crossing-out. What's more, mistakes in writing are instantly noticed by the reader – and are there for ever.

There are no 'ums' and 'ers' in writing, no false starts, no hesitant pauses or needless repetitions.

You would be unlikely to find words like 'yeah' and 'sort of' and other conversational words in writing (unless, of course, they were inside inverted commas as quoted speech).

You can edit what you write, polishing it until you get it just right, but you can't easily edit what you say.

135

Writing is mobile in space (you can carry this page around with you) and in time (these words were written long before you read them – and someone else may read them next week, next month, next year . . .). Unless electricity is used, speech is restricted to the immediate vicinity of the speaker and to the immediate present.

Different social functions

Most people spend far more of their lives talking than writing.

People learn to talk early in their lives and without any formal training. However, everyone needs to be taught how to use written language and this process of teaching and learning takes many years.

The ability to write and to read come later than speaking in the language development of individuals as well as whole societies. Millions of people in the world today cannot read or write. Many human societies are largely illiterate. There are still many adults in Britain who are, for all useful purposes, unable to read and write.

Writing is often used for communicating things which matter, things which the writer has really worked hard to express in the best possible way and which, therefore, he or she wants to preserve.

Until certain things are written down, they don't carry the same significance, the same 'weight of truth' as when they remain spoken. Legal documents, for example, and Holy Writ, are examples of the added authority of writing over speech. By implication, 'my word is my bond' means that spoken assurances should carry the same weight as if they had been written down.

For all these and other reasons, writing well is more than simply knowing how to reproduce the spelling and punctuation of the writing code; it also involves being aware of the social characteristics of written language, characteristics which differ from those of speech.

Writing in college

Writing in college is also a social situation: one in which you are communicating something to at least one other person

136

through your writing. In fact, it is a highly specialised social situation in which reading and writing become a daily activity, part of the fabric of the whole experience. Most people read and write far more in college than they will ever do for the rest of their lives. Furthermore, writing in college is carefully controlled, monitored and assessed.

Therefore, one of the most important skills you will need to practise is how to make your written style match the expectations and requirements of your college reader. Since, as you have seen in 'Who are you writing for?', this reader is likely to be your lecturer, and since he or she will be approaching your writing as an expert in a particular academic or vocational study, this implies that the style you are aiming for is the style of the subject you are writing about. Once you can define that, you have a model in which to write. And that makes your task easier than if you were aiming for something you couldn't properly see.

Register

Learning a subject is, to a great extent, learning how to use the characteristic language style of that subject – its 'register'. People who are expert in their subject not only know its facts and relationships, its processes and practices; they also know its language. This language may differ only slightly from the language of the layman or it might display considerable differences (for example, in the use of technical vocabulary) which only those well-versed in the subject can understand. Learning to write successfully in college, then, must include learning how to use this specialised language. Of course, all the important conventions of written language (spelling, punctuation, clarity of structure, etc) remain constant no matter what you are writing about. However, it would be quite inappropriate to write about geography, for instance, in *exactly* the same way that you would write about physics or history or economic theory; and the variations from that constant, the *particular* stylistic characteristics of the subject's language, constitute its register.

It's a language which you will assimilate in part from those who are learning with you and from your lecturers. It may take a while to acquire and feel at home with this language, but the more you practise it, the more quickly you will come to use it naturally and successfully, making it your own. One important way to find the right register is, of course, in your reading. If you are reading the books and articles associated with your subject, you will learn much more than simply the facts and ideas inside them: you will begin to learn the appropriate style of writing in which your subject is normally expressed.

Register (like style generally) can be described in terms of the language used and the social attitudes within it. What kinds of words tend to be used in the register? (Does a chemist talk about 'precipitate' or 'the sludge at the bottom of a flask'?) What sorts of sentences tend to be used? (Do scientists prefer: 'The mixture was heated' or 'We get hold of a bunsen burner and, once we had managed to find some matches, heated the stuff up in a flask until the air was quite unbreathable, and then went out for a couple of beers'?) How is the reader addressed in geography – as a person ('You'd have been astonished at the incredible scenery we saw when we were up in those mountains!') or the anonymous reader ('The terrain gave evidence of glaciation.')? When writing a critical essay in English, do you try to stand back from the experience of reading the book ('Twain tried to organise the reader's reaction to the America of the mid-nineteenth century by letting him see everything through the eyes of an innocent child.') or do you gush ('Twain is fantastically brilliant the way he tries to get us to question everything we see about life on the Mississippi by letting it all come out of the mouth of Huck Finn who is only a child.')? Do you (as one writer did) express the intensity of the love which one character feels towards another like this: 'The trouble with Jude was that he loved her. He truly, truly loved her!' or, a little more objectively, like this: 'Jude's problem lay in the intensity of his love for her'?

Effective style in writing – that is, writing which most directly communicates the meaning of the person who uses it to the person or people who read it – conforms to the habits of the register in question. It is appropriate.

You will find your own written style in college is more closely under control if you keep in mind the question: is the way I'm writing this appropriate? Appropriate to the subject about which I'm writing? Appropriate to the context in which I'm writing it? Appropriate to the requirements and expectations of my readers?

Your own voice

So far, we have seen that style in writing is not the same as style in speaking; that style consists not only of the language used but also of the social attitudes which this language communicates; and that these social attitudes must be appropriate to the context in which you are writing if the style is to be successful.

We have also seen that college is itself a specialised social context and that, within college, there are the many even more specialised contexts of the subjects themselves, each with its own particular language characteristics or 'register'.

Where, in all this, is your *own* voice? Is it possible to be yourself when you write, or should you try to suppress your own personality as it comes through your writing in favour of the (perhaps) rather anonymous 'voice of the subject'?

Referring to your reader

How, for example, should you address your reader? Which way is the most appropriate? You will have noticed that this book often uses the word 'you'. In certain kinds of writing, this makes the language more direct than if you were addressed impersonally as 'the reader' or 'students' or 'users of this book'. However, the way you address your reader depends on the functions you are trying to fulfil in your writing. In the kind of writing you will do on your course, you are less likely to want to address your reader personally.

Remember *who* you are writing for: someone who is trying to help you learn and who is also given the responsibility of assessing your work against the standards of others. Furthermore, although you are writing particularly for your lecturer, there is also a sense in which you write for an *unknown* reader, that anonymous but interested person who shares a concern for your subject (who may even know quite a bit about it) and who might one day pick up your writing and read. Too personal a style of address restricts the writing in this case, and that anonymous stranger may therefore feel he or she is reading writing meant for someone else.

Also remember *what* you are writing for: to sort out your thoughts; to show what you know; to demonstrate that you can think about it in a sensible, reasoned way; to persuade a reader of your point of view; to bring an argument to a conclusion. Writing of this kind can often benefit from a cool, dispassionate approach in which too much personal address would be inappropriate.

Referring to 'ourselves'

One stylistic feature of much academic writing is the use of the word 'we':

> We have seen that . . .
>
> Having looked at X, we can now proceed to investigate Y.
>
> Where before we were concerned with A, we must now turn to B.

Generally, the use of 'we' in this context reminds the reader of the *community* of scholars who are, together, engaged in the study of the subject concerned. It is based on the assumption that both the writer and the readers are members of the same group, bound together in their shared interest in the topic.

At a less academic level, the use of 'we' also tries to mark the connection between 'I' as the writer and 'you' as the readers. (The implication is that there are probably more than one of you out there; except in a letter, a writer using 'we' in a personal conversation with a single reader is a little on the cosy side.) Because 'we' is less direct than those other pronouns, a less intimate connection is made, which includes but does not smother. Especially in the context of academic writing, 'we' can be a useful device for trying to keep your readers with you as you wend your way through the different points of an argument. It works at the half-way point between the completely impersonal (where neither writer nor reader are mentioned at all) or the intentionally de-personalised ('the reader will have noticed . . .' 'the present author has often maintained that . . .') and the direct address which, as argued above, may seem to lack the necessary objectivity for academic writing. 'We' can hold the middle ground. It is as intimate or public as the reader wishes to make it, as appropriate in the secret paragraphs of a personal letter as in the packed benches of a lecture hall.

Be careful, though, of using it when expressing opinion:

> Having read X, we are inevitably of the view that . . .

140

may leave some of your readers complaining, 'Wait a minute! *You* may be of the view, but *I* don't agree at all!'

Referring to yourself

However, don't be afraid of 'I'! So many students have been told at school that they should never use the word. 'Your writing must be objective, dispassionate, impersonal,' they are told; so the direct statement of a personal opinion or feeling becomes almost an act of defiance. This need not and should not be the case. It is far better to write, 'I have been reading so-and-so . . .' than 'the present writer has been reading so-and-so' or even 'so-and-so has been read'! If you believe something as a result of your thinking, then why not admit it? 'Having considered such-and-such, my own view is that . . .' is a clear statement of the fact that you, personally, have come to hold an opinion. There's no harm in saying so.

Writing about yourself

Referring to yourself as 'I' is not the same thing as bringing yourself too much into your writing in other ways. It is the case that writing for a course of study tends to require the student to be objective and not to display too much personal emotional involvement. In many subjects, it is rare for emotional involvement to become an issue. In others, however, it may. Perhaps the most extreme example is to be found in the writing of critical essays in English. Because the subject of the writing has often started off as the genuine involvement of the writers in a book or play or poem which has impressed them, they sometimes feel impelled to communicate how *moved* or *excited* they have been when reading it. This could be dangerous!

Knowing how far to go is partly a matter of experience. The student who wrote: 'He loved her. He truly, truly loved her!' shows us a case of the written voice approaching too closely the spoken one and this is inappropriate in the context of a college essay. While she could have made such a statement in conversation, it didn't work in the writing because it was too passionate, too insistent. Her lecturer would have wanted to say, 'All right! I believe you – no need to shout!' With more experience, she learned to quieten things down and as a result her point of view became more, not less, powerfully-expressed.

There is no reason why your own excitement, if you feel it, should not be expressed quietly, in the background, rather than being forced on the reader. Your lecturer will certainly want you to be absorbed and excited by the subject. But he or she will prefer to know how far you are able to stand back from this involvement and view the subject clearly than to be impressed at the nature of your soul. In cases like this, it's not bad advice to recall Wordsworth's phrase 'emotion recollected in tranquillity' when you come to start writing.

Formal and informal

Don't be too formal. Many student assignments hit a false note because the writer seems to feel he or she needs to use as many long and obscure words, as many well-rounded and 'scholarly' phrases, as possible. Because you are writing an assignment in an academic setting doesn't mean you have to wear a gown and mortar-board. Instead, look at the style of a writer in your subject whom you really admire, whose work you find exciting and powerful and hard to put down; the chances are that none of these features will be present. Good writing makes its point with the least fuss. So can yours. Pretending to a style because you think it may be more impressive is a good way to make what you write seem pretentious and hollow. Better to be direct and simple.

However, you needn't go too far in the other direction and wear your oldest jeans. Don't be too chatty. You are not writing a letter to a friend when you write an assignment for your lecturer. Writing in this context is a far more formalised undertaking than is a friendly letter, in the same way that it is quite unlike talking in conversation.

*

To end with, take hope from the fact that lecturers can themselves be guilty of bad style. This extract, from a report on a college course, shows how easy it is to let the spoken voice creep in unawares and take the writing by surprise:

> However, in general the individual comments included under Section D showed fairly clearly that the comments were quite

142

often to a large extent rather irrelevant in that they were based on errors or misconceptions relative to the central theme of what the session was all about.

Notice the phrases *'fairly* clearly','*quite* often' and '*rather* irrelevant'. Are the italicised words necessary? They would sound quite natural in speech, but in writing they give the impression that the writer is less than precise in what he wants to say. Two other phrases – 'in general' and 'to a large extent' – suggest the same imprecision. Put together, the five phrases blur the meaning expressed: everything is qualified, toned-down, blunted. There's also an unnecessary repetition in ' . . . the individual comments . . . the comments were . . .' suggesting that the writer was forgetting words written only a few moments before: '*they* were' would have been more successful.

The last part of the sentence is too wordy: 'relative to' means the same as 'about'. And is there really any need to write both 'the central theme' and 'what the session was all about' since they, too, mean the same thing?

Here's the extract tidied-up: you can see how leaving out some words and phrases, and reorganising others, helps to achieve a clearer written style.

> However, individual comments in Section D were often irrelevant because they were based on errors or misconceptions about the central theme of the session.

The original example shows a writer who is only half-aware of the way he is using words. This was probably because he was very busy, dashing off his report without paying much attention to its style. He might respond to the criticisms above by saying, 'Look – I haven't got time to think about the fine details. What matters is the basic idea, and that – surely – comes across clearly enough. I'm writing a report, not a work of literature!' However, the style of a report needs to be as appropriate to report-writing as the style of a novel needs to be to novel-writing. Reports must be clear, but the style here obscures rather than clarifies the meaning.

A writer's 'basic ideas' are best expressed when the style of writing is *appropriate*. The language must be appropriate to both the content (the 'basic idea') and to the needs and expectations of the readers. Where these are out of balance, the style is unsuccessful and so reader and content are kept apart. (In the example above, it was the reader's need for simple

143

clarity which was not being considered.) So when you write in college, keep in mind the relationship between the *matter* of your writing and the *manner* in which you write it. If you fail to relate these two, your style will work against the ideas you are trying to express. Keep them in harmony, and your reader can come closer to the things you want to say.

Quotations, references and bibliographies

◆

Completing assignments requires a rather specialised kind of writing. It means that you need to observe certain conventions if your lecturer is to be satisfied. One such convention – really quite a sensible one – demands that you acknowledge what you have read in your writing.

This is done in two ways: through 'references' and in a 'bibliography'. The first makes sure that, at each point you mention someone else's writing, either quoted directly or referred to in your own words, you acknowledge as much. The second is to list all the books and articles in which these references first occurred at the end of your assignment.

The precise way to satisfy these demands is a matter of debate among those for whom it is a regular part of their working lives. Lecturers will even meet in committee to decide on a 'departmental style' in such matters. (Some promising professional relationships have been known to fracture as a result of disagreement.) Your own lecturers may give you a hand-out at the beginning of your course in which they show how they prefer students to reference work and set out a bibliography. If so, use it. Their preferences are likely to be as good as anyone else's. If, however, you are offered no help, this chapter gives suggestions you should find useful.

Whatever you do, you should not underestimate the importance of references and bibliographies. The story is sometimes told of the student who had his assignment returned by a lecturer with only two words written at the end: 'Punctuation.

Fail'. When he asked how his punctuation could be so bad as to have led to complete failure, his lecturer replied, 'But you forget to put the quotation marks at the beginning and the end.'

By failing properly to acknowledge your reading, you stand in danger of being accused of the most serious of all academic sins: 'plagiarism'. Plagiarism – copying other people's writing (including your friends') and passing it off as your own – is a kind of theft, and most lecturers will take a very serious view of it. If, at the end of your course, it is proved that you have plagiarised other people's work, it is very difficult for an examinations board to do anything else but fail you altogether. After all, they cannot easily offer you a final grade since they have little evidence of work which is your own. At best, they will assume you are simply naive. ('But I didn't realise we had to *say* we were quoting from a book!') and at worst they will know you are a cheat.

That, of course, is the negative reason for observing the conventions. The positive reasons are that, in studying a subject, you are attempting to enter a society of ideas and knowledge, the members of which communicate with each other largely through the articles and books they write on that subject. So when you come to write an assignment, your lecturer will want to see which ideas, and which members of the community, you have been considering in coming to your own point of view.

Many students start a course thinking that an assignment must be 'all their own work' and that to confess they have sought inspiration from books is a sign of defeat – as if they couldn't think of enough to fill out an essay with ideas of their own. This is understandable, especially when each is being urged to 'think for yourself!' and where high praise is awarded for 'originality'. However, it is mistaken. An assignment is usually the place where you bring together all the learning you have been doing in its preparation, shaping it into a written text to be read by someone – your lecturer – who is more experienced. He or she will want to read your own ideas, certainly, but will be equally concerned to see how you have arrived at them. Where this involves reading, as it almost certainly will, giving evidence for that reading is completely appropriate and you should not feel reluctant in doing so. (If you aren't convinced, look at the daunting bibliographies which so often accompany learned articles in the library in

which the authors seem positively to boast about how many books they have read.)

Quotation and referencing

There are two ways you will use other people's words in your own writing: by 'direct quotation' and by 'indirect quotation' in which you rephrase what they say into your own words. In each case, you should acknowledge the fact in a 'reference'.

Quotations are straightforward. If they are comparatively brief – say, less than two lines long – then put them in single inverted commas within the text itself. If they are more substantial, give them a paragraph to themselves and indent the whole quotation. In this case, you don't need to use inverted commas. (Both kinds are shown in examples below.)

Whichever kind of quotation you decide upon, you will need to reference it, and this is where different systems are preferred by different writers. The simplest is just to write a number in brackets after the reference or quotation and then give details either in a footnote or at the end.

Slightly more explicit is the 'Harvard' system, in which you write the surname of the author you quote, together with the year of publication of the book or article from which you are quoting, in brackets immediately afterwards:

> In studying the anatomy and brains of early man, Huxley came to a conclusion which Herbert Wendt reminds us was 'at the time considered highly provocative but which is now obvious to every anthropologist' (Wendt, 1974).

Later, you will have to say some more. Either in a footnote at the bottom of the same page, or alternatively at the end of the essay, in a section labelled 'References', you will need to give these details:

> Wendt, H *From Ape to Adam* (1974) – p. 71

You could, of course, put this kind of detail in the essay itself:

> In studying the anatomy and brains of early man, Huxley came to a conclusion which Herbert Wendt reminds us was 'at the time considered highly provocative but which is now obvious to every anthropologist' (Wendt, H *From Ape to Adam* (1974) – p. 71).

but you may think this clogs your writing. Whichever way you

147

choose, however, such detail will be required if you are to do the job of referencing properly.

Sometimes, you will be quoting from an article or a chapter written by one author which appears in a book edited by another. Here, you should reference as follows:

> Children learn to label their world partly by labelling large categories and then learning how to name the things within them. As Brown reminds us:
>
>> The dog out on the lawn is not only a *dog* but is also a *boxer*, a *quadruped*, an *animate being*; it is the *landlord's dog*, named *Prince* (Brown, 1958).
>
> This opens up some interesting problems for us about how a person's vocabulary grows in relation to the world around them.

Then, in your footnote or your reference section:

> Brown, R: 'How shall a thing be called?' in Oldfield, R & Marshall, J (eds) *Language* (1970) – p. 82

Alternatively, the article you quote from may not be found in a book edited by another person but in a magazine or journal. In that case, write the reference like this:

> Sale, R: 'Four Studies in Impatience' in *Citations* (No. 91) – p. 32

There are times when you might want to quote from another book by the same author. That's when the date is particularly helpful: it distinguishes the two books. Later, in your bibliography, you will be listing the full titles of each one, so no more than the date is needed within the essay itself. And if, by chance, the writer has written more than one book in the same year and you want to quote from each, write the reference as, for instance, (Johnson, 1980:b).

If you quote on more than one occasion from the same book, then you can make use of the term *op. cit.* This means 'in the above-mentioned work' and it saves you re-stating the author and date at each reference or quotation. Instead you can write:

> Sarlcott 1979 – p. 34

and later on the same page

> *op. cit.* – p. 45

Naturally, this becomes impossible if another author intervenes between these two references in your list. But a fuller

148

version can still be used, depending on the style you adopt for your references:

Sarlcott, R *British Infantry Regiments* (1979) – p. 45

then references to different authors, and then:

Sarlcott: *op. cit.* – p. 70

If you refer more than once to a particular passage in a book, then you could use another Latin abbreviation in the same way: *ibid.* ('in the same place').

Ibid. – p. 34

Ibid means that the second reference occurs on the same page.

If referring to a point would mean that you would have to cite a great many references to the same book (because the book is full of references to the same idea) you can use the term *passim*:

Sarlcott (1979), *passim*

but you should normally try to be more precise. For instance, if a reference first occurs on page 34 but is then repeated many times during the same chapter, you could use *ff*:

Sarlcott (1979) – pp. 34 ff

With indirect quotations, exactly the same thing applies. You may, of course, rephrase into your own words something you have read in a book or article, only now you will need to use your discretion a little more. The first example above could, for instance, be rewritten like this:

> In studying the anatomy and brains of early man, Huxley came to a conclusion which Herbert Wendt reminds us (Wendt, 1974 – p. 71) was considered very provocative at the time but which anthropologists today see as being obvious.

You can see that the words have changed, though their essential meaning remains the same. Nonetheless, you are strengthening, not weakening, the force of what you write by letting your reader know that you are drawing attention here to an authority who has written on the subject, even though the words are becoming ever more your own. Compare that with:

> In studying the anatomy and brains of early man, Huxley came to a conclusion which people then thought was provocative but which all anthropologists think is obvious today.

Here, your lecturer might decide to ask you: 'On what basis do you make such as statement? Where's your evidence?' Alternatively, he or she may recall a passage from Herbert Wendt's book on the subject, look it up and discover that you are saying virtually the same thing, but not admitting it.

Quotation, then, is not always an exact matter. It exists on a gradient, from direct quotation at one end:

> 'Precisely because the pseudosphere is actually bigger than the plane, it is very hard to represent in the normal Euclidian space of our drawings.' (Rucker, 1986 – p. 103)

to a close re-statement where, although there is no direct quotation, the words follow the original almost exactly:

> Rudy Rucker tells us that it is precisely because the pseudo-sphere is actually bigger than the plane that it is so hard to represent in the normal Euclidean space of our drawings (Rucker, 1986 – p. 103).

to a restatement in your own words at the other:

> Within the dimensions of our drawings (normal Euclidean space) drawing a pseudosphere is going to pose us with considerable difficulties. That's because it is so much bigger than the plane of our drawing. We'd need to shrink it first.

By this stage, it would be reasonable to argue that the ideas had become your own (especially because of the last sentence) and that therefore no reference is needed. Nonetheless, there is no harm in reminding your lecturer that this idea has emerged in your own mind from having read Rudy Rucker's book *The Fourth Dimension and How to Get There* (Penguin, 1986). So a good compromise would be to remind him as follows:

> Within the dimensions of our drawings (normal Euclidian space) drawing a pseudosphere is going to pose us considerable difficulties. That's because it is so much bigger than the plane of our drawing. We'd need to shrink it first. (See Rucker, 1986 – p. 103.)

Use your discretion. But err on the safe side. It is far better to give references than not to, if only to avoid the risk of being thought to have used other people's ideas as if they were your own. What's more, it shows your lecturer that you are alive to the literature of your subject and have done some reading!

Here's a page of references from a student writing his dissertation (on the revolutionary movement in England between 1792 and 1820) in the final year of his history degree course. Coming at the end of his degree, and in a long study, it is much more substantial than were the references in his other assignments. These references, for the third chapter of his study, each refer to a numbered note in the text itself. They come, together with all the others, at the end of the complete assignment. Notice how, once he has listed the author and title of a book once, he can repeat it in subsequent references using the (time-saving) *op. cit.* You will also find *ibid.* and *passim*. (The abbreviation (ed) means 'editor'.)

3. Bread or Blood (pages 12–18)
1. Hutchinson, T (ed) <u>Poetical Works</u> – p. 165
2. Christie, I. R <u>Stress & Stability</u> – p. 30
3. Stevenson, J <u>Popular Disturbances</u> – p. 92 (table 5.1)
4. Thomis, M. I & Holt, P <u>Threats of Revolution</u> – p. 78
5. Christie op. cit. – p. 215
6. Williams, R <u>Culture & Society</u> – p. 33
7. Collins, H (ed) <u>Rights of Man</u> – p. 133
8. Burke, E <u>Reflections on the French Revolution</u>– p. 63
9. Collins op. cit. – p. 68
10. <u>Annual Register (1790)</u> – Preface p. iii
11. Burke op. cit. – p. 53
12. op. cit. – p. 82
13. op. cit. – p. 76
14. op. cit. – p. 83
15. <u>ibid.</u>
16. op. cit. – p. 84
17. op. cit. – p. 83
18. op. cit. – p. 63
19. Williams op. cit. – p. 24
20. Cole, G. D. H & Filson, A. W (eds) <u>British Working Class Movements</u> – p. 124
21. Hobsbawm, E. J <u>Labouring Men</u> – p. 2
22. Collins op. cit. – p. 187
23. op. cit. – p. 106
24. op. cit. – p. 194
25. op. cit. – p. 196
26. <u>Gentleman's Magazine</u> (1799 – Part I) – p. 867
27. Thompson, E. P <u>The Making of the English Working Class</u> – p. 117
28. op. cit. – p. 19
29. Cole & Filson op. cit. – p. 24
30. Silver, H <u>English Education & the Radicals</u> – p. 11
31. Thompson op. cit. – p. 175

32. Thale, M (ed) <u>Autobiography of Francis Place</u> – p. 196
33. <u>op. cit.</u> – p. 128
34. <u>op. cit.</u> – p. 139
35. <u>op. cit.</u> – p. 155
36. <u>op. cit.</u> – p. 144
37. Williams, M (ed) <u>Revolutions</u> – p. 124
38. Thale <u>op. cit.</u> – p. 148
39. Stevenson <u>op. cit.</u> – p. 129
40. Thompson <u>op. cit.</u> – p. 72
41. Stevenson <u>ibid.</u>
42. <u>op. cit.</u> – p. 134
43. Thompson <u>op. cit.</u> – p. 183
44. <u>The Times</u> April 21st 1797
45. Stevenson <u>op. cit.</u> – p. 149
46. Thompson <u>ibid.</u>
47. Christie <u>op. cit.</u> – pp. 3–26
48. Thompson <u>op. cit.</u> – p. 484
49. Burke <u>op. cit.</u> – p. 52
50. Thompson <u>op. cit.</u> – p. 184
51. Elliott, M <u>The Despard Conspiracy Reconsidered</u> – p. 53
52. Colley, L <u>The Apotheosis of George III</u> – passim
53. Stevenson <u>op. cit.</u> – p. 142
54. Colley <u>op. cit.</u> – p. 194
55. Thompson <u>op. cit.</u> – p. 194
56. Collins <u>op. cit.</u> – p. 295
57. Christie <u>op. cit.</u> – p. 54

This list of references took a long time to compile, partly because the writer had not kept sufficiently clear notes as he went along of all the books and articles he had read in preparing for the dissertation. Avoid this if you can. It can take hours to search back through a book for that quotation you vaguely remember being on a left-hand page somewhere near the beginning. (This is even harder to do if you find that someone else has taken the book out of the library.) Far better would have been to note the reference (perhaps on file index cards) as you do your reading. References can then be compiled quickly and easily. (See 'Making notes'.)

Bibliographies

By the time you finish your essay, you should already have listed – either in footnotes, in a section called 'References', or in the text itself – all the references you have made in terms of an author, a date of publication and a page number. Now comes the time to collect together all the publications from which these references have been taken. A bibliography lists all the books and other materials you have referred to in writing your assignment. The normal way to set out items in the bibliography is like this:

Author's surname, initial *Title* Publisher (Date)*

Put each item on a different line, working in alphabetical order.

Borris, F   *Freedom and Absurdity* Mayes Hill (1967)
Charmers, T   *Absurdity & the Law* Grunewaldt (1973)
Erikson, P   *Legal Absurdities* Sparrow (1982)

List books by the same writer in date order:

Frome, W   *Understanding Astrology* Midget Press (1981)
      ,,   *Look to the Stars!* Midget Press (1982)
      ,,   *Your Future in the Sky* Midget Press (1984)

You have already seen that an article within another book should be set out as follows:

Bernice, S 'The Fellowship of Rooks' in Galstone, P and Medway, G (eds) *Essays from Eagle Mountain* Fleetway House (1979)

If you are using sources of different kinds, then list them as above but within labelled sections. First, list any *unpublished* works (for example, letters). Next, list *published works*, broken down into three sections: (i) books; (ii) articles; (iii) newspapers, magazines, etc.

Here's the bibliography from the same history study. There are no unpublished works so the only sections used are in the 'published' category.

BIBLIOGRAPHY

Books

Burke, E *Reflections on the French Revolution & other essays* Everyman's Library (1910)
Christie, I. R *Stress and Stability in Late 18th Century Britain: reflections on the British avoidance of Revolution – the Ford Lectures* Clarendon Press (1984)

---

*An alternative layout is:
    Author's surname, initial (date) *Title* Publisher

Cole, G. D. H & Filson, A. W (eds) *British Working Class Movements 1790–1870* Macmillan (1965)

Collins, H (ed) *The Rights of Man: Tom Paine* Pelican (1969)

Hobsbawm, E. J *Labouring Men: Studies in the History of Labour* Weidenfeld & Nicholson (1968)

Silver, H *English Education & the Radicals 1780–1850* R.K.P (1975)

Stevenson, J *Popular Disturbances in England: 1700–1870* Longman (1979)

Thale, M (ed) *Autobiography of Francis Place* C.U.P (1972)

Thomis, M. I & Holt, P *Threats of Revolution in Britain: 1789–1848* Macmillan (1977)

Thompson, E. P *The Making of the English Working Class* Pelican (1968)

Williams, M (ed) *Revolutions: 1775–1830* Open University (1971)

Williams, R. *Culture & Society: 1780–1950* Pelican (1961)

Articles

Briggs, A 'Middle-class Consciousness in English Politics: 1780–1846' in *Past & Present: 9* (1956)

Colley, L 'The Apotheosis of George III' in *Past & Present: 102* (Feb. 1984)

Elliott, M 'The Despard Conspiracy Reconsidered' in *Past & Present: 75* (May 1977)

Newspapers, etc.

Annual Register (for 1790)

Gentleman's Magazine (for 1799)

The Times Newspaper (for April 1797)

One word of warning. Once students recognise that their lecturers like to see bibliographies, they often overdo things. They find all the books they can think of which are concerned with the topic of their assignment and list each one – never having referred to half of them in the essay itself. Don't do this! Only list books you have referred to or quoted from; any other titles on your bibliography will cause your lecturer to ask, 'Why is this title listed when I can find no reference whatever to the book in the essay itself?' This is a kind of academic name-dropping, not far removed from showing off, a pretence at reading you have not really done. Stick to the books you have actually used. And if you have read more books on the topic than you have referred to or quoted from in your writing, then by all means list them (set out in just the same way) under the separate heading: 'Background reading'.

*

A final point. It is surprising how often people mix up the words 'quote' and 'quotation'. Very common in a student's assignment is to read: 'This quote shows us that . . .'. The correct word in this context is 'quotation' – the noun. Only the verb is 'quote' – in just the same way that you may 'invite' someone to a party. An 'invitation' may be referred to by some as 'an invite', but only, one hopes, in informal conversation. (After all, you would not refer to a reference as 'a refer'.) Such small points may seem pernickety, but they all help to make the right impression upon readers who, as the years go by, may become increasingly irritated by what they regard as the abuse of the language by their students.

Using a
word-processor

————————◆————————

A word-processor, if you are lucky enough to have access to one, can be a powerfully useful writing tool. For more and more students, writing assignments on a word-processor is becoming the norm rather than the exception. There are great benefits to be gained from learning how to use a word-processor. But there are some dangers too.

What is a word-processor?

In case you are unfamiliar with the technology of word-processors, here is a brief description of a typical word-processor system such as you may learn to use in college or may have seen in other people's homes.

Home word-processors look modest enough: a keyboard, which looks like a slim-line typewriter, a VDU (Visual Display Unit), which looks like a TV set and which allows you to see on the screen what you are typing; and a printer, which looks like a typewriter without the keyboard. The word-processing program is run in a computer rather as a tape recorder will play a cassette: you simply load in the program, or call it up from a microchip within the computer itself, and start writing. (The computer can, of course, do all kinds of other things as well – from playing games to working out the family budget.) If you want to save what you have written after you have switched off the power to the computer – perhaps because you want to come back and write some more next day – you will need some kind of electronic storage. In the early days of home computers, this used to take the form of a tape cassette machine. Now the use of floppy disks is almost universal.

The difference between a word-processor and a typewriter is that, with the former, you have much greater control over the words you are typing. Most obviously, you can immediately correct spelling or typing errors without using Tippex – you simply move the cursor on the screen to the incorrect letters and type the right ones in their place. In fact many word-processing programs include a spelling checker which actually matches each word you type against the words stored in its memory, alerting you if it cannot find a match and so giving you the chance to alter your word to the correctly-spelled version. It will even suggest alternative spellings from which you can choose.

If correcting spelling was all that word-processors could do, they would not be worth the money they cost. But you can achieve much more complex things with them which, for many writers, makes them cheap at the price. For example, you can mark a section of writing and then move it to another part of the text; or delete it altogether; or import a piece of writing, perhaps from an earlier version of your text, into the piece of writing currently in the machine. You can, in this way, edit your work more or less indefinitely (a process which, on a typewriter, would require you to start each sheet of paper from the beginning in order to end up with a clean, error-free copy).

You may decide that you would like to insert some writing, anything from a single letter to a whole chapter. On a word-processor, this is easy. As you type in the new insertion, all the writing below will move down to make space. You can change a word, reorganise a sentence, swap the order of paragraphs – all at the touch of a few keys on the keyboard.

What's more, you can often do things with the characters on the screen – for example, make them appear in **bold** face, or *italic* script. You can set up neat columns, easy-to-read tables, perfectly centred and underlined headings and, until you decide that you have your text exactly as you want it, nothing need appear on the paper itself. Printing comes last of all: the final moment of satisfaction after the hard work of composition. With a word-processor, you have complete control over your writing.

But then – so you do with a pencil and an exercise book.

The word-processor cannot do your writing for you. What it

can do is to take much of the hard work out of composing and editing so that, in theory at least, your mind can be released for the more important things involved in writing: thinking up ideas and expressing them in the best possible ways. Where, with the older ways of writing, the mechanical processes necessary for translating these ideas into clean, crisply-printed paper were often laborious and time-consuming, with a word-processor the production of high-quality text is simple and efficient. A word-processor allows you to present nonsense to professional standards.

So think hard before you decide to use a word-processor for doing college assignments. For example, can you type? If not, you will have to spend some time learning – time which could perhaps be better spent in reading. Are you good with technology? If not, you will need to spend some time in familiarising yourself with the basic procedures involved in word-processing. These are not difficult to learn but you will nonetheless need to develop some simple habits if you are to avoid problems. (Using a word-processor is rather like driving a car: once you know what you're doing, it becomes second nature, but learning can take a little while.)

If you are not sure whether to start learning, here are some pros and cons to consider.

Disadvantages

- Word-processors are very expensive. Buying your own could use up a year's grant. Furthermore, they use electricity (though not much) which must be paid for.
- If the college provides word-processing facilities, make sure they are readily available. It can be annoying to have to wait hours or even days before you can book time to write that extra section in your assignment which you thought of last night in the bath.
- Using them 'fluently' takes time to learn.
- They are not very portable. You have to go to them, whereas you can carry paper and pens around anywhere. This becomes particularly important if you need to be close to books when you write your assignment: few college libraries will allow you to plug in the several bulky pieces of electrical equipment needed for word-processing (though you can buy battery-driven portables called

'lap-tops'). Of course, many college libraries increasingly provide microcomputing facilities with word-processing software included.

- Making alterations in what you write can become obsessive. You may reach the stage of never being satisfied. Where, with other forms of writing, the process of making changes eventually becomes too laborious, forcing you to finish and be done with it, word-processing can tempt you into trying just one more alternative. In consequence, some pieces of writing never get finished.
- A momentary lapse of concentration can sometimes mean accidentally deleting your writing in the time it takes to press a button. The same effect can occur if there is a sudden power-cut. Hours of work can vanish in a nanosecond. (You have to go through this experience at least once in your life to realise fully the meaning of the word 'despair'.)
- The technology stresses presentation rather than content.

Advantages

- Language errors – as long as you can recognise them – are easily eliminated. Gone are the days of typing mistakes!
- You will be able to produce well-presented assignments which can often create a better impression on the reader than pages of script.
- The process of *composing* becomes more active and controllable. For example, you can quickly sketch out the main sections of a piece of writing, then add sub-headings for sub-sections, then begin to write opening and closing sentences for each one, all without committing yourself. If you want to change things, you can do so at once.
- The process of *editing* becomes more controllable as well. You can easily *add, subtract, reorganise* and *refine* your writing, testing and evaluating the changes you make as you go along, until you are completely satisfied.
- You can store your writing very conveniently, disks being far less bulky than files of paper and capable of holding a great deal of writing. (The contents of this book, for example, can be stored on just one 3.5-inch disk.) If you are concerned about the effects on the natural environ-

ment of destroying trees to make paper, you may prefer
to store your writing on plastic.
- Once you become an accomplished user, you may well
  find that you write more quickly on a word-processor
  than in any other way.

Will it make me a better writer?

This is the most important question you should ask about
word-processing. Assuming that you have achieved mastery
over the technology itself, you should find that the extra
control word-processors give you over your writing provides
greater freedom over your ideas. Since ideas are, to a considerable extent, no more nor less than the language which expresses them, it follows that the more control you have over this
language, the more power you will exert over your ideas. It is
above all in *composing* that some people have found word-
processors to be a liberation. To use the keyboard/screen
combination as an electronic scribble-pad is an improvement
(some would say a quantum leap) over the back-of-an-
envelope collection of ideas – if only because you can so easily
move, change, delete and add to the ideas you sketch out as
you gaze thoughtfully at your VDU, your fingers playing over
the keys.

People who use word-processors regularly look back to 'The
Time Before' with a slight sense of guilt. They know that so
much of what they wrote then did not benefit from the same
process of polishing because that process took so long. With a
word-processor, there's really no excuse for not getting your
writing to the point of perfection. That's a heavy responsibility.

*

A note on technological progress. At the time of writing,
word-processing itself is beginning to become a little out-of-
date. New computer programs are coming onto the market
which complement and extend the possibilities of word-
processing software. 'Document processors' and 'Desktop
publishing systems' allow you to do all the things which
word-processors will do, while at the same time paying particular attention to the visual qualities of the finished text.
Print-styles can be manipulated with great precision. Because

certain subjects (mathematics, for example) require specialised symbols, such software can be very useful, allowing you to design symbols to suit your own requirements. Desktop publishing programs will also allow you to alter the print styles you use, set up columns of text, use banner headlines, draw pictures and diagrams – in fact do most of the things which it would have taken a professional typesetter to achieve before their invention. They are useful for producing brochures, college newspapers, advertising sheets, etc. The term 'desktop publishing' is a little ambitious: these programs cannot yet manufacture texts and make them commercially available (though who knows . . .?). With a high-quality printer, however, it is already possible to prepare print to the stage of 'camera ready copy' (pages which are ready to go to a printer to be made into books).

But before you buy one, consider whether your college assignments are ready – just yet – to hit the bookstalls.

Getting it back

———————◆———————

You hand in your work. You wait. Time goes by. Then, your lecturer gives it back. What now . . . ?

Lecturers will differ in their techniques for marking assignments. Some will return your writing with another essay attached – the pages of notes they have written in response to your work. Others will write nothing at all. (A student was once a little taken aback on the return of her dissertation – a 20,000-word masterpiece which had taken three months to write – to find no more on it than a faint pencilled tick in the bottom right-hand corner of the final sheet.)

You may receive a written grade (either numerical or 'literal' – a letter of the alphabet) but it is just as likely that you will not. Some lecturers won't give grades on principle: they believe their written comments are what matter and that grades introduce an inappropriate aspect of competitiveness into what ought to be a purely educational experience. (This can lead students to ask: 'Yes – but how did I *do*?') Sometimes, lecturers are *not allowed* to give grades or marks. The regulations governing the assessment and examination of students' work may strictly forbid it on the grounds that, until the final examinations board has ultimately considered each student's performance at the end of a course, no mark or grade can have any validity and that therefore students may not know how well, or badly, they have done (an interesting argument). However, it is probable that lecturers will nonetheless record a grade for their own use, especially in a course which is continuously assessed.

Other lecturers feel that the awarding of a grade can save the need for other written comments. ('B+ says it all, surely!') If it is the practice on your course to be awarded a literal grade, this may come 'pure' or 'adjusted'. Pure grades are simply letters of the alphabet – 'A' meaning 'excellent', 'B' 'good', 'C' 'average', 'D' signifying 'below average' and 'E' meaning 'poor'.

Adjusted grades show a lecturer trying hard to be more precise in his or her judgement. 'A−' or 'C+' suggest assignments that are 'just a little way from being excellent' and 'rather above average but not yet good' respectively. Lecturers who find it hard to be decisive can sometimes agonise for long periods about whether an essay is genuinely a 'B−(+)' or a 'C++(−)'. Or maybe they are only trying to be scrupulously fair.

All this, of course, raises questions: 'good' against which standard? Is there some kind of general standard, or one which applies only to the individual student? In the latter case, it could be that a student is awarded an 'A' yet still produces work which is lower in standard than the 'C' of someone who is better at the subject. If you aren't certain, ask your lecturer to explain. For instance, is the time you have been on the course taken into account? Does an 'A' grade at the start of a course mean the same as an 'A' grade shortly before the final exams? It is surprising how rarely lecturers tell their students on what basis they will be assessed, but this may be because they are never asked. If you are puzzled about the assessment criteria operated on your course, ask. It is very hard for anyone to succeed if they are unsure on what basis success is to be judged.

The time to get worried is when your literal grades begin to explore the middle reaches of the alphabet. If you start getting 'F', 'G' or 'H' grades, think seriously about changing your lecturer. Or your course. The record low is probably a mark given to someone who could manage only a single word in a Latin translation paper – 'taurus'. He wrote 'bull' in the middle of a page otherwise empty but for his name and received a grade of 'G minus to the power seven'.

Obviously your grades will matter to you. But do not let them become an obsession. At least one student in the USA, disgruntled by the fact that his professor of mathematics had given him no more than a 'C' grade for an assignment, shot him in the chest: some might say a rather petulant reaction. If you are uncertain about why you have been given the grade you have, once again: *ask*! If the comments on your assignment do not in themselves make it perfectly clear, then the lecturer will tell you orally – though you should be prepared in some cases for some home truths.

In fact, he or she is likely to want to talk to you about your work in any case, and may set aside time for just such a purpose. After all, you are writing for much more than just the acquisition of a grade; the main reason is because writing helps you in learning the subject you have chosen to study. Therefore, disappointing though it may be to receive a low grade, try to see it as part of the learning process: an indication of how to get a better one next time. And if you are in the fortunate position of receiving a high grade, use that as an indicator for the next assignment you write. What did you do which you could profitably repeat?

Ideally, your lecturer will have supported the final grade with a commentary of remarks throughout your work. (Remember to leave enough room on the page for them: most important, and often neglected.) However, if these comments are sparse, it could be that your lecturer intends to report back to you mainly in conversation. For that reason, the written comments may be very brief – memory-joggers which he or she expects to speak to you about later.

Above all, think of your writing as a particularly detailed part of a longer, wider dialogue with your lecturer. Faced with a class of students, it is impossible for him or her to deal with each one individually, but this ceases to be the case when assessing your writing. It is only here that a lecturer can really come close to the fine detail of your thinking and understanding. For this reason, if for no other, you should attend carefully to the comments you will find on your assignments, using them as the basis for progress to the next stage of your learning. They are your lecturer's best means of helping you to get better still.

Writing in examinations

———— ◆ ————

This book cannot guarantee you pass examinations but it may show you a way of making the best use of what you know on those pressured, nerve-racking occasions. In the end, how well you know your subject will almost certainly determine whether you pass or fail. But a well-written answer could make a crucial difference. Examiners' reports frequently refer to candidates' powers of written expression (or lack of them), complaining about poor spelling, inadequate or absent punctuation, clumsy grammar, poor phraseology and other 'assaults upon the language'.

Examiners are almost human

There are examples of exam questions which can be marked by computer, but for the present purposes assume your examiner displays almost normal human characteristics: tiredness, impatience and so on. He or she will do the best job possible in reading and marking your exam answer accurately and fairly, but if your paper is an 'assault upon the language', or if it irritates in some other way, you cannot wholly blame the examiner if he or she finds it difficult to admire.

The examiner cannot judge how well you know your subject if, for example, absence of punctuation obscures your meaning or if a combination of weak spelling and poor handwriting (a particular problem in the rush to complete exams) renders part of your answer unintelligible.

Clarity of communication resides, however, not only in the smaller units of words, phrases and sentences but also in the

167

overall organisation of your answers. So you need to persuade the examiner not only that you know your subject, but also that you can argue a point of view, give a clear and complete account, describe or recount with precision. It is not the examiner's job to try to guess what you *may* have wanted to say.

Much of what is said elsewhere in this book should help you to tackle at least some of the problems that are mentioned here – spelling, for example. But some of the points below are related to the particular nature of exams and the pressures and circumstances that inevitably come with them.

Read the rubric

The comments below may seem so obvious as to insult the intelligence of the readers of this book. They certainly aren't meant to. They are all based on things which candidates commonly do in exams, things which harm their chances of success.

'Rubric' is another word for 'instructions'. Help the examiner (and so help yourself) by following the instructions that are given in the exam paper. Some of these concern the questions; others the general administration of the exam itself. Together, these instructions make up the rubric of the paper. One complaint of examiners is that candidates 'don't read the rubric'.

The rubric will tell you how many questions you should answer and from which sections they must come. Allow yourself a few moments to understand the rubric so that you know exactly what you should be answering. It may help to mark the questions you intend to answer and then to check that you have followed the rubric about which are and are not open to you in a given section. It is pointless to throw away marks simply because you ignored instructions. (People do, though.)

Other parts of the rubric concern the administrative side of the examination. Bear in mind that your answers may be marked by a number of different people, according to the questions set. If you're asked to start each one on a new sheet, or in a new answer book, then do so. Few things will infuriate an examiner more than having to wait for another examiner to finish marking, simply because your answers on 'Tourism in the South East' are in the answer book that should have been reserved for 'Tourism and the Law'.

For the same reason, write your full name on each answer book or sheet of paper, plus any other details that will help to identify your script. Exam sheets, in their hundreds, are often tied together with string. One false move and page three of your second answer might find itself lost in the general pile on the examiner's desk. Without your name on it, this could prove a handicap.

If you are using answer books, check that you have completed all the details on the cover of each one you use, including such details as 'centre number', 'candidate number', 'course title' or whatever is appropriate. Also, fill in the box on the front cover (if there is one) which shows which questions you have answered and in what order.

Presentation

Writing an exam answer is a little like applying for a job. The interviewer or appointments committee forms a first impression of you from your letter of application – what you say and how you say it. So with examinations: impressions do count. Some candidates seem to think that the pressure of exams gives them licence to be as untidy as they please and that, somehow, the examiner will assume that under normal circumstances they are the very model of orderliness. But the exam paper is your *only* contact with the examiner, your *only* chance to convince him or her that you should pass. Therefore you need to care about the impression you convey. This is all part of considering the needs of your reader.

Timing

Before you go into the exam room, you will probably know how much time you should be able to give each question. Your lecturers ought to be able to help you here by telling you the format of the paper before the exam. It may be the case that certain questions carry more marks than others and, if so, they will probably have told you this as well. You'll need to plan your timing accordingly. This may seem so obvious as not to merit mentioning here. However, you'd be surprised at how many exam candidates spoil their chances by miscalculating time.

Take, as an example, a three-hour exam where you have to answer four questions with 25 marks per answer. In order to reach the pass mark (which is often 40 per cent), you need to get an average of at least 10 marks for each question. If you complete all four questions reasonably, you'll reach 40 per cent – a bare pass. If you write nothing for the fourth question, however, you've failed because your possible total is now only 30 per cent. Writing three answers means that you could pass only if you improved your standard on them to at least 13.5 – and that's a big jump from 10 in terms of what you would have to write. Better would have been to attempt that fourth question and try to build up your marks that way, rather than struggling on with three questions in the hope of getting the extra marks.

The same thing applies when you aren't struggling. One question may come up on which you know you can write brilliantly. Do so – but not at the expense of the other three. In the four-question exam, no single answer can carry more than 25 per cent and if you spend most of your time polishing your best answer to perfection at the expense of all the others, even the most generously-inclined examiner can do little more than give you full marks for that one question – still leaving 15 per cent to find to achieve a bare pass.

But what happens if, despite your plans, you're running out of time for question four? All is not lost. Give your examiner an idea of what you would have written by showing a skeleton plan – the main ideas of the answer, the arguments for and against the case, etc. Show him or her that you *could* have written the answer very well had it not been for lack of time. It's certainly not a strategy to be recommended for every exam you take, but most examiners will not be entirely unsympathetic if they see from the other three answers that you genuinely mis-timed yourself on the fourth and so they may give you some marks for question four.

Planning

Elsewhere, this book stresses the importance of careful planning before you start writing. However, one way of wasting

170

time in an exam is to take too much time for planning. Exams are different from your term-time writing and what may be appropriate then is neither appropriate nor feasible now. It is one thing to jot down a few main headings and perhaps a concluding sentence or two to guide you in your thinking; quite another to draw up an elaborate plan. Such planning is time-consuming and may have to be abandoned as the minutes tick by.

You have seen elsewhere that different kinds of writing require different kinds of structure. By the time you come to take your exam, you should be in a position to recognise the type of structure that is needed and this should help make your fast mental planning more efficient.

Select

If you know your work well, you should be able to approach your exam questions swiftly, confidently and with a good idea of the areas to be included in a particular answer. This does not, of course, mean writing down everything you know. Still less does it mean writing down the model answer you practised the night before the exam. *Answer what you have been asked.* No matter how good your practice answer may have been, if it doesn't answer the question, it cannot really be awarded any marks at all.

You are not supposed to be demonstrating to the examiner that you know *everything* there is to know on a particular subject. What you should be doing is showing how you can select from the breadth and depth of your knowledge and understanding to answer the particular question asked. Your exam answer should show the broad outlines, fill in all the necessary details, and persuade the examiner that this answer, though excellent in its own right, is merely part of what you know, a judicious and appropriate selection from what you have in stock.

Checking

Though spending too much time planning is not to be recommended, it will be worth leaving around five minutes per question to check through what you have written afterwards.

Particularly because you will be writing in a hurry, all kinds of errors (of spelling and punctuation, but of more substantial things as well, like leaving out words or writing incomplete sentences) tend to occur without your noticing. So check. The corrections you will probably find yourself making to each answer in those few minutes at the end could well raise your grade.

Practise!

One brilliant undergraduate student did miserably in his final exams for the simple reason that he had spent three years of his course writing assignments on the typewriter. When he came into the exam room and found he had to hand-write everything, he was lost. He should have practised.

There are two reasons why it makes good sense to practise writing exam answers. Firstly, it gets you used to framing what you want to say in a fixed period of time. Like training for a race, you will begin to know when half the time is up . . . when you only have 10 minutes left . . . when you should be bringing things to a conclusion . . . when you ought to be going on to the next question. If you haven't practised in this way, the circumstances of the exam itself may throw you entirely off course and mental effort which should be going into showing what you know is wasted in making sense of the context itself.

The second reason is that it will give you confidence. Assuming you have done your revision and know what you know well, then to spend three hours answering unseen questions on this knowledge can actually be quite exhilarating – providing you have done your training first. If only for this reason, revision should include writing of practice answers against the clock. These answers can either be taken from past exam papers or ones which you have set yourself.

In fact, setting yourself some likely questions is a good form of revision. After all, most subjects are already broken down for you into particular areas during your course. Once you remove those questions from each area that you know you *won't* be asked (because they were on last year's paper, or because you already did an assignment on them as part of your coursework) you will usually find that there are not too many more which even the most obscure examiner could think up for you. What's more, the process of asking yourself: 'What are the likely questions on this topic?' is a very good way of organising your mind to do the necessary revision.

Don't panic!

Above all, don't panic! Very few people really *enjoy* exams. It is difficult to be cool-headed when you know how much is at stake and when you are writing against the clock. But remember that examinations never try to catch you out with trick questions (for what would be the point?). They aim to allow you to show two things: what you know and how well you undersand it; and your ability to write intelligently and coherently on an aspect of the topic without knowing in advance precisely what that aspect will be.

In both cases, you can prepare yourself for the experience and, if you are well-prepared, there should be no need for panic at all.

ENDPIECE

Writing assignments on a college course should not be a sequence of disconnected events but a coherent, developing *process*. It generally accompanies your studies throughout, as well as being the usual means by which you submit your work for assessment and formal examination.

This book has been about how to prepare yourself for writing in either context: forming a positive attitude; making effective preparations; feeling confident within the writing system itself; and being able to work within some of the special conventions expected of people who write in college and for an academic readership.

Writing assignments in college should never be a mechanical exercise, undertaken only to satisfy the demands of the assessment schedule of your course. It is an active process: a transaction you make with your readers, be they the 'educated non-specialist' who may one day read what you write, the community of others who are studying your subject and who may read your work with more than casual interest, or your lecturers themselves. As well as your responsibility to them, remember theirs to you: to use your writing not only to assure themselves of the growing quality of your work, but also to help you move your studies to their next stage. So the last skill to learn, and the most important of all, is the readiness to listen carefully to constructive criticism.

Finally, remember that other reader who will read your work with more attention than any, if only because he or she will realise how much thought and care has been given to its preparation. Whatever you write, this reader can be your sternest critic as well as your most enthusiastic champion. That's because writing in college is, above all, the process of communicating with *yourself* about your growing knowledge and understanding and the deepening pattern of your ideas. The most important reader of all, therefore, is you.